"This meditation on the Our Father is vintage Shea: theologically astute, spiritually alert, deeply attuned to the needs and aspirations of the human heart. Anyone interested in cultivating a more intentional relationship to God should read this book."

— Bishop Robert Barron
    Auxiliary Bishop of the Archdiocese of Los Angeles

"John Shea is fooling us—like always. He is not just helping us open to the Our Father as a transformative spiritual practice. He is providing a richly detailed, deep, comprehensive understanding of Spirit and how we can savor imagination, vulnerablity, joy, social action, faith, and communion in order to travel the path of spiritual development."

— Mike Carotta, religious educator,
    author of *Unexpected Occasions of Grace*

"Jesus left us one prayer as the root for all prayer, the Our Father. In this marvelous, very readable book, John Shea shows us how that prayer is embedded in our very DNA and how it can bring God's presence into every moment in our lives, from saying 'good night' to each other to standing at others' death beds. A great read. Few authors write with the depth of John Shea."

— Ronald Rolheiser, OMI, is president of the Oblate School of
    Theology in San Antonio, Texas

D0684264

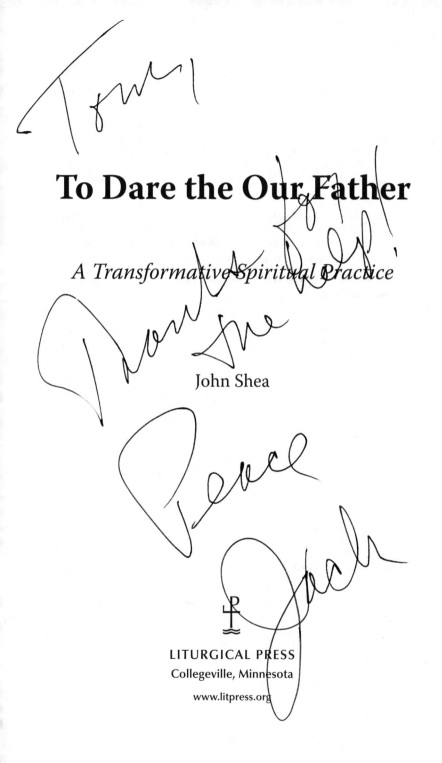

To Dare the Our Father

A Transformative Spiritual Practice

John Shea

LITURGICAL PRESS
Collegeville, Minnesota
www.litpress.org

1	2	3	4	5	6	7	8	9

Library of Congress Cataloging-in-Publication Data

Names: Shea, John, 1941– author.
Title: To dare the Our Father : a transformative spiritual practice / John Shea.
Description: Collegeville, Minnesota : Liturgical Press, 2018.
Identifiers: LCCN 2017035867 (print) | LCCN 2017048158 (ebook) | ISBN 9780814645857 (ebook) | ISBN 9780814645604
Subjects: LCSH: Prayer—Christianity. | Lord's prayer. | Spiritual life—Catholic Church. | Catholic Church—Doctrines.
Classification: LCC BV210.3 (ebook) | LCC BV210.3 .S49 2018 (print) | DDC 242/.722—dc23
LC record available at https://lccn.loc.gov/2017035867

To All
Who have prayed the Our Father
Who are praying the Our Father
Who will pray the Our Father

Contents

A Personal Preface

This is *not* a book about the Our Father/Lord's Prayer (two titles for the same set of words). It is a book about praying the Our Father/Lord's Prayer so that it transforms how we think, will, feel, and act. These transformations open us to the ultimate Source of life, facilitate the flow of Spirit in and through us, and enable us to carry out the agenda of the prayer. Although praying the Our Father is commonplace Christian fare, praying it as a transformative spiritual practice is a more challenging undertaking.

The traditional invitation to the Our Father—"We dare to say"—is correct.[1] This prayer is a series of spiritual and social imperatives. To take it on is to be initiated into a vocation that, even as it remains a mystery, demands concrete changes in consciousness and behavior. I have been praying this prayer most of my life, and it is something I continually learn to do. Although I struggle with it in innumerable ways and do not completely live up to it, I have come to accept its dare as a life companion.

A Prayer for All Seasons

I have prayed the Our Father routinely and with great passion, in liturgical assemblies and in the anguished wakefulness of three a.m., with full-body participation and without moving my lips, in inner states of peace and in inner states of turmoil, in a slow, meditative frame of mind and rushing headlong for the last word. I have a history with this prayer, a history of confusion and clarity, of awe and boredom, of being unable to start it and being reluctant to finish it. But, most of all, my praying is an ongoing history and, with full Irish sentimentality, I hope to pray the Our Father or have it prayed for me at the hour of my death.

I grew up inundated with spiritual practices—Mass on Sunday and holy days, receiving Communion before daily Mass, monthly confession, the rosary, visits to the Blessed Sacrament, a catalog of prayers (Morning Offering, Act of Contrition, Acts of Faith, Hope, and Charity, etc.), Lenten fasting, May processions, spiritual reading, and meditation on gospel texts. As my life unfolded, I left behind many of these spiritual practices.

Practices that served me well in my youth often became the unwanted baggage of my middle years. Sometimes I dropped a spiritual practice because I realized it was reinforcing negative aspects of my personality. Sometimes I dropped a spiritual practice because its assumptions clashed with my present state of intellectual development. Sometimes a spiritual practice dropped me. I would return to it again and again, hoping to find fruit on its tree. I grieved that it was barren, and remembered past times when it filled me with spirit and love. I blamed myself and tried harder. To no avail. In the end, I had to bury it with honor.

I was relieved when I heard the Buddha's advice: you do not need to carry the canoe once you have crossed the river.

It put a positive spin on my history of shedding spiritual practices. The abandoned practices had done their work: they had helped me cross the rivers that needed crossing. They may no longer be relevant, but they had fulfilled their mission. Other practices were now needed. But whatever interpretations are brought forward to describe my on-again off-again affairs with spiritual practices, the fact is there are many abandoned canoes in my wake.

However, I did not let go of the Lord's Prayer. It is a canoe I have paddled since my youth and still do. It has survived the purification of my inherited spiritual practices, and I do not think I am alone. For many Christians, the Lord's Prayer/ Our Father accompanies their lives. When they are happy or when they are sad, when they eagerly wait for a child to be born or silently stay as an elder dies, when they hear of a plane going down or attend a church going up, when they stroll alone in the woods or gather together in Christian assembly, when they are filled with gratitude or emptied by grief, when they are driven to praise or dragged to repent, they reach for the Lord's Prayer. It is a prayer they know; the familiar words are on their lips. The Our Father has become an all-purpose prayer, a prayer for all seasons.

But it is not a prayer for all seasons because it suits every occasion. It is not topical. The Christian tradition has produced a multitude of prayers for specific situations—marriages, deaths, anniversaries, graduations, weather, victories, births, homecomings, traveling, healings, sufferings, desired outcomes of all kinds, and so on. Since God is the ultimate reality who contextualizes and permeates every individual happening, human imagination and creativity calls upon God to become an actor in those situations or calls upon the human players to become aware of the presence and activity of God in those situations. The words of these prayers are situation-specific;

and some of the most gifted Christian wordsmiths have crafted beautiful and moving meditations.[2]

But the Our Father is person-specific. It identifies and strengthens the central Christian truth about the person in relationship to God and creation. This truth is always present. Although the prayer is not detailed and fine-tuned toward particular situations, it influences how we think, will, feel, and act in whatever situations we are in. This is an unsuspected relevancy. A particular situation challenges us with all its concrete pressures, and the last thing we think we need is to pray the Our Father. But if we do so with attention, the words take us down a path of insight and creativity, showing us possibilities we could not see without it. This has always been a surprise to me, but I have learned to both respect it and expect it. Remembering who we most deeply are makes the Lord's Prayer a prayer for all seasons. No matter what the season is, it is we who are experiencing it and it is we who are called to respond.

Some of the Seasons

If you ask my wife, Anne, what the best thing is that has happened in our marriage, she will say, "Praying together." I agree, but I am not as forthcoming about it. Every night, as a prelude to sleep, we pray together the Our Father. If we are not together at the end of the day, we connect by phone to make this end-of-day ritual happen. Once we prayed the Our Father while I was at a session break in California and she was walking down a relatively deserted street in downtown Chicago. We do not sleep until the Our Father has brought us together.

We alternate phrases. If Anne begins, "Our Father," I follow with "who art in heaven," and she continues with "hallowed be thy name." We are off and running, our bed or phone connection a chapel of antiphonal prayer. When the prayer is over, we pray for all our friends and everyone in the world who is severely challenged. Connecting the Our Father to solace and betterment for all we know and know about seems right.

In 1995, my father, John, was in Lutheran General Hospital. The doctors had put him in a drug-induced coma. They hoped that would give the antibiotics time to work and check the blood infection that was coursing through his body. Although my father was eighty-two years old, they were optimistic.

My mother and I had just come from her doctor who had prescribed, at her request, some antianxiety medication. As we exited the elevator on the ninth floor of the hospital, a pastoral care person met us. I do not remember what she said. But as soon as I saw her, I knew my father was dead.

My mother and I went into the room where his body was. My older sister was already there. My father's head was back and his mouth was open. Mercifully, his eyes were closed. We stood around the bed, stared at our father and husband, and stared at one another. Cried. Instinctively, we took each other's hands and said the Our Father. My sister said, "Daddy's no longer here. Let's go."

Eleven years later, my mother, Ann, was in Oak Park Hospital. She had suffered a massive stroke. My two sisters, my wife and I, and some of our mother's grandchildren spent about a week sitting by her bedside. One night my wife and I left at about ten. We lived only three miles from the hospital. As we opened the door to our condominium, the telephone rang. I picked it up and the voice of a young woman simply said, "Miss Ann passed."

We contacted everyone and returned to the hospital. We stood around our mother's body, looked at her and one another. Cried. We instinctively held hands and prayed the Our Father.

When I facilitated groups of faith reflection, I would often ask, "What is your favorite part of the Mass?" After someone got the easy laugh with "the end," people would be silent. They were taking time to work with some internal evaluation process. When the answers finally came, a wide range of liturgical moments was usually mentioned. The theologically appropriate and probably most correct "hearing the word of God" and "receiving Communion" were always mentioned. But so were "the Creed," "the homily (sometimes)," and "the kiss of peace." Also, a surprising contender was "saying the Our Father together."

The harder question that followed was, "Why is that your favorite part?" People were not as articulate with this question, but a common characteristic was that at their favorite part of the liturgy their participation sharpened. There was a heightened engagement, a sense that they were included in something larger and important. This response was more affective and intuitive than carefully reasoned. It was discovering a preference rather than selecting something desirable. I assume that this question would be answered in different ways at different times and, in particular, at different ages. When we are young, one way; as we age, another.

Recently, when I have asked the question of myself, I have found that the combination of the "saying the Our Father and the kiss of peace" comes to mind. The two seem to flow into one another and are part of a single movement. When I asked myself why, I found myself tracing my history with the Our Father. What I discovered was that saying the Our Father was a practice I often engaged in but usually took for granted. Doing it in a community liturgy and finding myself deeply attached to it pushed me to reflect more on how it was working in my life. Moving toward others with peace from the consciousness of that prayer was an unfolding with which I was familiar. Something happens to me in that prayer that makes extending peace a natural and fulfilling expression.

Praying Alone

But it is not only in interpersonal and social settings, with people I love and with members of my church community, that I pray the Our Father. I pray it alone, an interior act of saying the words slowly and with as much sustained attention as I can manage. There is an irony in talking about praying alone a prayer that begins with the word "Our." Even when we pray the Our Father in solitude, we are not alone. Our praying participates in the monastic wisdom that the monk does not have to leave his room to be present to the whole world. It is this more leisurely time with the prayer that informs and enriches the more timetabled conditions of community prayer.

Praying the Our Father with other people always moves fast. Some have called it "speed praying." It is difficult to let the words sink in and have their effect on our minds, wills, and feelings. But if we have experiences of praying it privately, we can quickly import the meanings we have discovered during private time into the speed of the social settings. So, from my experience, personal alone time and social together time are partners in the project of Christian formation through the act of praying the Our Father.

But it was in praying alone that I became aware of difficulties that eventually pushed me into a deeper relationship with the prayer. I was saying the words of the Our Father and drawing blanks, nothing going on in my mind or will or feeling and no pictures of future behaviors beckoning to me. I could not get on board with what I was saying. Sometimes it was problems with the words and phrases. But at other times, a more structural questioning set in. I was not comfortable with the whole idea of petitioning. Requesting a transcendent and separate subject, imaged as a Father, to make things happen and give things to me and us, even when they are very desirable things and good for all, was an increasingly difficult "ask." At the time this is what I thought the words were forcing me into, a way of thinking that was increasingly less credible to me.

But at the same time, it seemed an "ask" built into me. Although my adult image thought asking for help seemed childish and unreal, my actual self was often quick to engage in it. Whenever I was in trouble, and even when I was not, I was prone to immediately recruit divine assistance. This instinct triumphed over rational resistance on a regular basis. I began to wonder if this tension would make praying the Our Father go the way of other practices. Did I need this canoe?

Praying and Studying

These types of tension—and this is only one of them— made me realize I had to *learn* to pray the Lord's Prayer. So I began to study. After all, the Lord's Prayer is the central prayer of the Christian tradition to which I belong and from which I seek resources to live an authentic life. It deserves a long and careful look. This study has taken me down scriptural, liturgical, theological, and spiritual paths. But it is driven by more than intellectual curiosity and academic interest.

Whatever I find in study I think is valuable and resonates with something deep inside me, I bring it into my act of praying. Under the impress of these learnings, my way of praying has changed and the imaginative phrases of the prayer have taken on new meanings. A particularly strong influence has been spiritual wisdom traditions, especially the writings of mystics and those who have been inspired by mystics. As I read them, I found they often articulated a cognitive-affective consciousness in a flurry of images and ideas. It was more abundant than precise, more a rich display than a sustained argument. Perhaps the prayer was a mystical text, seeded with a set of lures into different levels of consciousness—most importantly the mind of Christ?

This mystical guess gave me a new appreciation for the dense imagery and evocative phrases of the Lord's Prayer. Its sparseness was not a shortcoming but a way of demanding maximum engagement from those who would pray it. I never thought the Our Father was a pedestrian prayer. It had always left me with the feeling that my mind had not completely grasped what my mouth was saying. But now I began to see it as an invitation into a consciousness that was more fully developed than my normal structures of awareness. The mystery and elusiveness of the prayer was its teaching design.

But the more I entered into and entertained the mystical, the more I felt it pressured my interpersonal and social life. If these mystical appreciations were ultimate and, as ultimate, had a legitimate claim to call into question "how we do things around here," how did we measure up? So praying the Our Father became a dialogue between the mystical and the social with the surprising results that both reinforced and criticized each other.

Persevering

I was not sure I wanted all this. But I felt to back off was to walk away from something that was quintessentially real, even if I was "in over my head." Also I suspected if I did back off, it was something that would not go away and would eventually catch up with me. It is too dramatic to call it the "hound of heaven." But I did feel a sense of being pursued. Perhaps more apt, ala *The Godfather*, it felt like an offer I couldn't refuse. I caved and continued.

These dawning realizations caused the flow of my prayer act to slow down. I even allowed it to be interrupted and returned to, or interrupted and never returned to—at least not in the immediate prayer time in which the interruption occurred. In other words, consciousness was in the process of being altered and I was exploring its emerging perceptions and evaluating how to respond to them. I was following the thread through the labyrinth.

Praying the Our Father in this way includes pausing and reflecting when appropriate lures emerge. As such, it becomes an investigation of both hardened and flexible mental tendencies and the types of behaviors they validate. As I followed the calls in the praying, I was sent back to the act of praying with an expanded consciousness and, very often, a revised action agenda. Something was definitely afoot even if I was hard-pressed to give it a convincing name and a rationale of respectability.

In short, praying the Our Father became the way I consciously committed myself to life itself. My days were occupied with within-life dreams that were more or less realized and within-life strategies that were more or less effective. As I scrambled to get what I wanted, I brought this prayer about life itself with me. And surprisingly it had a lot to say about my dreams and strategies. It worked for me the way mountains work in spiritual literature. When we are on the mountain, we gain perspective. We see more, and we see it all interconnected. When we return to ground level, we try to act from the perspective that we had on the mountain. Many of the times I prayed the Our Father, it took me out of myself (mountain) and then returned me to myself (ground). The trip was well worth it. It is the backstory of this book.

A Transformative Spiritual Practice

Through praying and studying I gradually came to appreciate and engage the Our Father as a transformative spiritual practice. It was transformative because it gradually changed the way I thought and felt about myself and how I perceived and acted in situations. What the prayer seeks to transform is our conventional consciousness, our normal ways of thinking, willing, feeling, and acting, our take-it-for-granted convictions. In other words, it targets the mind and its ingrained habits. It was spiritual because with the mental changes came increased openness and cooperation with Spirit.

Spirit is not the effervescence of physical, psychological, or social experience. It is a dimension of reality with its own laws and operations. When our mental perceptions of this reality sharpen, we begin to risk its influences. We begin to dare the prayer. The game is afoot and we are following its tracks. This book is about the ins and outs of this experience of praying the Our Father as a transformative spiritual practice.

Chapter 1, "Praying Someone Else's Prayer: A Meditation Text," explores what is entailed when we pray a prayer that is not our own but one that is meant for us. It is the *Lord's* Prayer, but it is meant for his *followers* to say. As such, it is memorized and we have to deal with the mindlessness that often accompanies memorization. It also provides a harness that gives direction to thoughts and feelings. There is discipline involved. Christians recognize the legitimacy of extemporaneous praying, free-floating talk with and to God. But the Our Father is another type of prayer experience. It is basically a prayer of discipleship, inviting sustained attention and sharpened focus.

xx *To Dare the Our Father*

Therefore, it can be appreciated as a meditation text and engaged as a transformative spiritual practice.

Chapter 2, "Seven Challenges of Transformative Spiritual Practices," identifies some of the issues that are consistently present in engaging transformative spiritual practices—resistance, gradualness, integration, desire, expectations, compliance, and attention. Two teaching stories help us explore these issues that most likely will enter into our praying the Our Father, sometimes subtly and sometimes blatantly. That is why a spiritual teacher or director is often a savvy companion as we engage in a transformative spiritual practice. They have experienced these issues and can help us turn what could be obstacles into development possibilities.

Chapter 3, "Seven Challenges of Praying the Our Father," identifies issues of the Our Father when it is prayed within the Christian tradition of the imitation of Christ. They focus on the dynamic elements that are involved in making the mind of the prayer our mind. We have to understand and undertake the project of putting on the *mind* of Christ, trace the symbols into relevant meanings, use the prayer as religious motivation for social action, adapt petition language into a way of human openness rather than a way of asking for divine intervention, live comfortably on the continuum of faith, understanding, and realization, experiment with integrating behaviors consistent with the prayer, and pause to sync our mouth with our mind as we pray the words of the prescribed text.[3] If these distinctive challenges are not clarified and at least partially resolved, they generate confusion and undercut perseverance.

Chapter 4, "The Identity of the Ones Praying," describes who we are when we pray this prayer. The opening address, "Our Father who art in heaven," implies we are people of spiritual depth who have the chutzpah to call ultimate reality, in line with St. Paul, "Abba! Father!" This indicates the Divine

Spirit is generating our spirits and loving us into existence. This self-understanding has radical consequences, changing our consciousness on spiritual, psychological, physical, social, and cosmic dimensions. But we may not recognize ourselves in this description. It may be an identity with which we are not completely familiar and one which we have trouble accepting. Yet it is the first and most important of the transformations into which the Lord's Prayer invites us. So we must have some practices that help us make it our own. Nevertheless, at least for me, this identity is always a "formidable ask" and brings a dimension of daring into the whole prayer.

Chapter 5, "The Mission of the Ones Praying," examines the important imaginative move of bringing heaven to earth. This entails remembering and hallowing "thy name" on an earth that is prone to forgetting "Our Father who art in heaven," being committed to "[t]hy kingdom" of essential human dignity/common good on an earth of selective human dignity and dominating social arrangements, discerning "[t]hy will" on an earth where it is hidden in situations and cooperating with that will to maximize its influence. These phrases of the prayer state our commitments to the name, kingdom, and will of "Our Father who art in heaven." If this is what we are about, we naturally perceive the world through those commitments and begin to strategize how to act on them.

Chapter 6, "The Strategies of the Ones Praying," identifies the areas and issues of earthly concern. We are called to give bread in order to communicate love to vulnerable life, to forgive in order to find a new life beyond retaliation and reconcile the future, and resist temptation and evil as the way to center ourselves and act faithfully out of our true identity. Although no tactics are provided for these strategies, they impel us to engage many contemporary interpersonal and social situations. As we conclude the prayer, we may realize the purpose of our praying. In its promised way, the prayer is transforming our minds and releasing Spirit. We are becoming moment by stumbling moment disciples of the One who gave us the prayer.

Chapter 7, "Transformations and the Emergence of Spirit," is a summary of the seven transformations that we are invited into when we pray the Our Father. Through these transformations Spirit is released into our minds and bodies and elevates our interpersonal and social interactions. The previous chapters have explored this vision in detail, but the language of this summary contrasts the "before and after" of the transformations and envisions the emergence Spirit as a homecoming.

Some themes are reiterated throughout the chapters. But these are not needless repetitions. The book is a sustained and expanding reflection. Ideas that were developed in one context need to be further expanded in a new context in order for the flow of thought to build on what was previously established and move seamlessly forward. This is particularly the case with interpreting the prayer in terms of an identity, mission, and strategy that inspire the ones praying to create tactics for the concrete situations of their interpersonal and social lives. Hopefully, the outcome of this textured, multilayered approach is a coherent and consistent presentation of daring to pray the Our Father as a transformative spiritual practice.

Your Experience

Since this book is a reflection on my experience of praying the Our Father over many years, it does not propose anything normative. Nothing in this book is a model to be imitated. In fact, many theologians, scripture scholars, spiritual teachers/ directors, and committed Christians in general might object to this way of proceeding. Also, many of the ideas might need nuancing and even refutation. This makes the book what it is meant to be: a dialogue partner. Therefore, the best way to prepare to read its chapters and to interact with them is to recall your own history with the Lord's Prayer and the convictions, values, and behaviors it has generated and encouraged.

When did you first learn the Our Father and who taught it to you? What are the settings in which you pray it? When has praying it been a positive experience? a negative experience? a neutral experience? Are there some things about the content or process of the prayer that confuse you? Are you satisfied with praying it the way you always have? Are you open to thinking about new ways of praying it? Do times of praying it ever come to mind during the day as situations unfold and issues arise? Would you call the prayer a "companion" in any way? How does this prayer and how you pray it sync with other ways in which you pray? Is the whole idea of when and how to pray changing for you?

I always have been shaken by the maxim of the spiritual life that warned, "If you do not progress, you retrogress." It rules out standing still as an option; and that is an option my lethargy highly favors. My writing these reflections has been a way I have gone forward; I hope reading them will contribute to your going forward. Although the uniqueness of each of our paths has to be respected, spiritual development feels best when it is a joint venture.

A Companion Volume

Previously, I wrote four volumes on *The Spiritual Wisdom of the Gospels for Christian Preachers and Teachers.*[4] The first three supplied commentaries and teachings on the Sunday readings for Cycles A, B, and C. The last volume addressed the gospel readings that are recommended for feasts, funerals, and weddings.

This volume, *To Dare the Our Father: A Transformative Spiritual Practice*, can be a companion to those books. The imagery of the Our Father resonates throughout the four gospels. The more familiar we are with those texts, the more understanding and meaning we will bring to the prayer. The Our Father is a very compressed prayer. Unpacking its significance through gospel passages and then returning to its succinct form enriches both the prayer and the passages.

But the companion character of this book with the four previous volumes can often be more specific. When we attend Sunday liturgies, there is always a gospel passage to ponder and we always communally pray the Lord's Prayer. The two are not side-by-side, but they co-inhabit the same liturgical event.

Above, we talked about the "speed praying" that is endemic to community settings. In those situations, we cannot give prolonged attention to the phrases of the prayer. In fact, as we will see, every praying of the Our Father can facilitate a slightly different consciousness and can suggest slightly different consequences. Given this fact, the Sunday gospel can become an aid in praying the communal Sunday Lord's Prayer.

The gospel text for the Sunday may gloss one of the phrases of the prayer. Therefore, when we come to pray the Lord's Prayer, we can bring the meaning of that specific gospel to our attention and speaking. The brevity of the prayer is enhanced through the extended ideas and stories of the gospel. The Lord's Prayer and the good news about the Lord can complement one another. The four volumes of *The Spiritual Wisdom of the Gospels* and *To Dare the Our Father* go hand in hand.

CHAPTER I

Praying Someone Else's Prayer: A Meditation Text

To state the obvious, the Lord's Prayer is first and foremost the *Lord's* Prayer. Since there are two renditions of the Lord's Prayer in the gospels, a longer one in Matthew (6:9-13), which became the standard, and a shorter one in Luke (11:2-4), scholars are quick to conclude that it is the Lord's Prayer as remembered and reformulated by the Christian tradition. That is most probably the case, but our concern is not with the important historical work of moving from the actual Jesus to the scriptural witness. Even if the minds of many had some contribution to the final forming of the prayer, its "otherness" remains.

Of course, if we are followers of Jesus, we have not hijacked his prayer. Nor has the prayer been arbitrarily imposed on us by overbearing authorities. In the gospels, Jesus wants his followers to pray it. In Matthew's account, Jesus instructs the listeners to the Sermon on the Mount among whom his disciples are the closest to him (Matt 5:1), "This is how you are

1

to pray" (Matt 6:9). In Luke's account, the disciples pressure Jesus to teach them to pray "just as John [the Baptist] taught his disciples" (Luke 11:1). He responds with his prayer.

So the prayer may be Jesus', but it is also meant for anyone who would learn from him. It is not our creation, yet the Christian tradition, following the example of Jesus in the gospels, encourages us to say it. Therefore, it falls into the category of an inherited prayer; and the fate of inherited prayers is that they are memorized.

Memorization

Recently I was at a wedding reception where the minister was asked to say grace before meals. He began abruptly, "A man was being chased by a lion and came to a cliff. He had no way to escape and looked back to see the lion approaching. He decided to pray. Kneeling on the ground, he closed his eyes and prayed with all his heart. After a while, he opened his eyes. The lion was fifteen feet away. Much to his surprise, the lion was also kneeling and had his paws folded piously in prayer. The man strained to hear what the lion was saying. The words were familiar, especially to those assembled here tonight. The lion was saying . . ."

At this point the minister gestured for us to join in. Everyone prayed with gusto and without missing a beat. "Bless us, O Lord, and these your gifts, which we are about to receive from your bounty, through Christ our Lord." With little or no difficulty, the group was able to draw this traditional prayer out of the bank of memory.

If we were socialized into a Christian denomination, and I count myself among those who were, we most likely learned its prayers. We were taught prayers to say when we awoke and before we slept, before and after we ate, and at key times during worship services and liturgies. There were also special prayers—prayers of faith, hope, charity, contrition, praise, adoration, thanksgiving, and petition. Of course, at the center of all these Christian prayers is the Lord's Prayer, the Our Father. In the Christian tradition there is no shortage of prayers, and no shortage of Christian teachers eager to drill them into the next generation and applaud young minds for perfect recitation.

Many of us learned these prayers at a young age when memory could be effectively imprinted. Consequently, they have stayed with us. Even if we have not said them in years, in the proper setting we will get the words right. We can chime in with "grace before meals" when the minister gives the signal.

However, even if we have mastered the words of a prayer, it often remains someone else's prayer. We may never quite get into it. It may never express the thoughts of our minds or the feelings of our hearts. We say it more out of conditioning than genuine insight. We may say "Bless us, O Lord, and these your gifts, which we are about to receive from your bounty, through Christ our Lord." But we say it without gratitude and feel free to grumble about the poor quality of the food. The same rote recitation can happen with the Our Father.

Mystical Traditions

Mystical traditions are especially sensitive to this problem of saying inherited prayers without the corresponding interiority. In a classic Jewish story, "The Shepherd's Pipe," a villager does not take his son to synagogue services because the boy is too slow to learn the Hebrew prayers. Since he cannot learn the prayers, it is assumed he cannot worship. However, on the feast of the atonement the father brings him along. He is afraid if he leaves the boy alone, he will inadvertently eat and break the sacred fast. The father does not know that the boy has a shepherd's pipe hidden in the pocket of his jacket.

During the service the boy implores the father to let him play his pipe. The father refuses and finally grasps and tightly holds the pocket with the pipe. But the boy, driven by desire, wrests the pipe from his father's grip, puts it to his lips, and lets out a blast. The entire congregation is startled. The Baal Shem Tov, who is officiating at the service, tells the congregation that it was this spontaneous "blast from the pipe of the babe" that brought "all their prayers to the throne of God before the gates of heaven closed."[1]

One message of this simple yet profound tale is that genuine prayer comes from the center of one's being (symbolized by the shepherd's pipe). The boy does not know the inherited prayers. So he cannot use them. But he may sense that those who are using them are doing so ineffectively. The prayers are not reaching heaven because they are not coming from the center of the ones praying. There is a split between who they are and what they are saying. The problem is not the inherited Hebrew words themselves but the disjunction between these words and the interiority of the people saying them. The "blast from the pipe of the babe" is a unified action, bringing together inner awareness and outer expression.

One of Leo Tolstoy's mystical short stories illumines the same contrast between genuine spiritual expression and inherited prayers. A bishop, traveling by ship, is told that three hermits are living on a nearby island. He concludes that they are within his jurisdiction and, therefore, it is his duty to inspect their orthodoxy, so he persuades the captain of the ship to change course and put him ashore on the island. He finds the hermits and asks them if they are Christian. They wholeheartedly respond, "Yes!" He inquires how they pray and they tell him, "When we pray, we say, 'We are three. You are three. Have mercy on us.'" This unauthorized and perhaps heretical prayer horrifies the bishop. He quickly instructs them in the

Lord's Prayer, which he believes is the only proper way to pray if one is Christian. They do their best to learn the words, but they are not quick studies. Finally, the bishop returns to the ship satisfied he has done his duty.

Later that evening, while strolling on deck, the bishop sees a ball of light in the distance. As the ball of light draws closer to the ship, the bishop sees the three hermits are within it. They speak from within the sphere of light and tell the bishop they have forgotten some of the Lord's Prayer. They need him to reinstruct them. The bishop is jolted into a new level of awareness and awakened to the holiness of the hermits, a holiness that is more profound than the correct recitation of words. The humbled bishop merely says, "Go home and when you pray, say, 'You are three. We are three. Have mercy on us.'"[2]

Once again, genuine spiritual illumination is played off against memorized inherited prayer, in this case the central prayer of the Christian tradition. The hermits have found their own way of praying, and it obviously "works." They are enveloped in divine light, even though they cannot remember the Lord's Prayer that the bishop taught them. These two stories use conventional religiosity with its emphasis on correct formulas as a contrast to develop a more complete understanding of prayer. Prayer is not mere mouth material but the inner being of the human person in communion with God. Frederick Denison Maurice succinctly captured this tension: "The Paternoster [Our Father] . . . may be committed to memory quickly, but it is slowly learnt by heart."[3]

Extemporaneous Praying

This spiritual sensitivity to the difference between reciting prayers and genuinely praying can be developed in different directions. Sometimes it shortsightedly becomes a way to discredit the project of learning traditional prayers. If learning the prayers of someone else is prone to become mindless, why not move in another direction? People should pray out of their own hearts with their own words. In this way the words will always reflect the interiority of the one praying. Prayer will always be genuine and not the recitation of the words of another. The examples of the shepherd's pipe and the homegrown prayer of the hermits call us to follow the same original path.

This approach, however, has its own problems. We have many inner states, and the most panicky ones are the ones most prone to prayer. Our ego is always protecting and promoting itself, and prayer is one of its preferred strategies. We may feel the need to boast and sound like the Pharisee in the temple: "O God, I thank you that I am not like the rest of humanity—greedy, dishonest, adulterous" (Luke 18:11). Or we may be gripped by fear and pray, "Help, Lord!" Or we may feel grateful for our blessings and say, "Lord, thank you!" Or we may feel burdened by our circumstances and say, "Lord, why me?" Therefore, the problem is not that people do not pray. In fact, when a Gallup survey asked Americans about their spiritual practices in the last twenty-four hours, 67 percent of them said they had prayed. The problem is we are prayer machines, approaching God out of our ever-changing interior states. Free-floating prayer is just that—free-floating.

There is an indication St. Matthew knew this human tendency to pray out of whatever needful inner state presently possesses us. The Matthean Jesus warns, "Not everyone who says to me, 'Lord, Lord,' will enter the kingdom of heaven" (Matt 7:21). The "Lord, Lord" cries are the panicky outer expression of the sudden inner awareness of threat. In the same vein, he also criticizes an avalanche of words. "In praying, do not babble like the pagans, who think that they will be heard because of their many words. Do not be like them. Your Father knows what you need before you ask him" (Matt 6:7-8). It is going too far to say that we should not pray out of human need. But the tendency to engage in a garrulous recital of every physical and social want is definitely criticized.

In another passage, the Matthean Jesus develops this criticism:

> So do not worry and say, "What are we to eat?" or "What are we to drink?" or "What are we to wear?" All these things the pagans seek. Your heavenly Father knows that you need them all. But seek first the kingdom [of God] and his righteousness, and all these things will be given you besides. (Matt 6:31-33)

Our physical needs monopolize our awareness. We voice them to whoever will listen and whoever will help. There is a double danger when we bring our needs into prayer. First, we forget that God is an all-knowing care that does not need to be informed of our condition. Second, and more importantly, we do not seek first the kingdom. There simply is no room for kingdom consciousness and kingdom action. We are filled and consumed by need and petition. We cannot get beyond our urgent pleas, and the ultimate effect of their powerful hold on our consciousness is that the kingdom is in second place. Priorities have been lost.

A Meditation Text

So inherited prayers can become mindless recitations and personal prayers can reflect ever-shifting states of egocentric anxiety or bliss. The first misses the richness of the Our Father and the second bypasses the Lord's Prayer for whatever is currently capturing attention. Is there a prayer practice between these two actual but basically lower-level prayer possibilities?

One way is to engage the Our Father as a meditation text. This assumes the prayer has a "higher" mind than the ones praying; and the practice of praying it is to transfer this more evolved mind into the minds of the ones praying. This demands deliberativeness, a disciplined attention that offsets the tendencies to mindless recitals. The prayer is memorized, but the negative effects of memorization are countered by a steady, inner attention. This mindfulness allows us to pray the words in a way that is in tune with their level of awareness, to pray them on their own terms, so to speak.

As a meditation text, the Our Father also provides a harness that is by no means a straitjacket. It charts channels for thoughts and feelings, and it encourages exploration. But it does not allow the mind to jump from thought to thought and feeling to feeling, turning each into prayer material. In this way the prayer quiets our incessant needs and opens for us to the reality that the gospels think is truly first, a first so inclusive that within it all our needs are strangely and surprisingly met.

Perhaps most importantly, when we engage the Our Father as a meditation text, we give it a chance to perform its purpose, the task for which it was designed. The Our Father is meant to pass on the mind of Christ by creating mental perceptions in the ones who pray it. For many reasons these perceptions are not easy to understand; and, for those same reasons and more, these perceptions are even harder to establish as permanent features of consciousness. However, their ultimate goal is not merely a changed mind. This changed mind is meant to see possibilities of action that previously it could not envision and to engage those actions and their consequences. This makes the Our Father a prayer of discipleship, and in order to achieve that purpose it has to become a transformative spiritual practice.

CHAPTER 2

Seven Challenges of Transformative Spiritual Practices

I had a friend who often finished his advice, advice he was very fond of giving, with "Be warned!" He was a believer in foreknowledge. If we knew what was coming, we would be better prepared to meet it. It is hard to argue against this—except that what we think will happen seldom happens in exactly the way we think. This is especially true when we undertake learning to pray the Our Father as a transformative practice. It is more in the nature of an adventure than of executing a well-thought-out plan. However prescient we are at seeing some things coming, we will not completely eliminate surprises and our stumbling attempts to respond to them.

However, the more we know about practices that seek to be transformative, the more we might see opportunities, tolerate difficulties, and stay the course as we engage in one practice—praying the Our Father. In order to gain some advance knowledge about the experience of these types of practices, we will consult two stories. The first story is "Finding New Eyes." It is the recounting of a surgeon's progress by Rachel Naomi Remen and has all the marks of our contemporary secular/spiritual culture. I will trace the basic plotline, but reading the full story is highly recommended.[1] There is much more in the story than I bring out. The second story is "Turning the Wheel." It is ultimately from the Islamic/Sufi spiritual tradition, but the version we will consult has been slightly modified.[2] It is a symbolic narrative of how transformative spiritual practices do and do not work.

We will draw seven challenges of transformative practices from these two stories. The stories narrate concrete situations, but the implication is these situations are not unique to the stories. These situations, or ones very similar to them, occur frequently. Although it is not surefire that these situations will come up in every transformative spiritual practice, they have a reputation of appearing over and over again. When they do, we are forced to adopt an attitude toward them and engage in strategic behaviors in order to work with them. This is why they are challenges. They come with the territory of transformative spiritual practices and insist, "Deal with me!"

"Finding New Eyes": A Contemporary Story of a Transformative Spiritual Practice

A brilliant but depressed surgeon visited Rachel Remen for help. He was seriously thinking about early retirement. "I can barely make myself get out of bed most mornings. . . . I hear the same complaints day after day, I see the same diseases over and over again." Remen suggested a spiritual practice—journaling the events of the day. In the evening he should revisit the day from a new perspective, in particular, recalling the day through three questions:

"What surprised me today?"

"What moved me or touched me today?"

"What inspired me today?"

The surgeon was reluctant, and part of the reason seemed to be he was too busy to carve out fifteen minutes for personal work. He was in the school of "how can my life be so busy and yet so empty?" Remen encouraged him. "Less expensive than Prozac," she said. Laughing, he agreed to try.

At first, working with these questions was disappointing in the extreme. He called Rachel and "sounded irritated." "Rachel, I have done this for three days now and the answer [to those questions] is always the same: 'Nothing. Nothing and nothing.' I don't like to fail at things. Is there a trick to this?"

Rachel gave him some advice. "Try looking at the people around you as if you were a novelist . . . or maybe a poet. Look for the stories." Even with this suggestion, at first he only saw the familiar material of his work in an unfamiliar way. Tumors that are not typical and experimental drugs that work in unexpected ways were what surprised him. "But gradually he had begun to see more deeply. Eventually he saw people who had found their way through great pain and darkness by following a thread of love, people who had sacrificed parts of their bodies to affirm the value of being alive, people who had found ways to triumph over pain, suffering, and even death." He began to see the people along with their disease.

But, as he began to see people, he was only able to see them in hindsight. At night when the day was done, he would look back through the eyeglasses of his three questions and see what he could not see when he was in the midst of it. But, then, gradually he began to see the inspiring, the moving, and the surprising as it was happening. This was major growth for him and made possible the next step. He began to say what he saw. He talked about more than the disease. He talked to people about their minds and spirits as they walked with their sickness. The practice had produced an inner change, and now the inner change was producing a behavioral change.

Remen comments, "Most of us lead far more meaningful lives than we know. Often meaning is not about doing things differently; it is about seeing the familiar things in new ways. When we find new eyes, the unsuspected blessing in work we have done for many years may take us completely by surprise." In other words, if the mind can change and open, it can receive the Spirit that is present.

Three Challenges from "Finding New Eyes"

Resistance

When the surgeon's work turned sour and he found himself in a numbing rut, he immediately thinks the problem is in the outer world. His work is the culprit. So he begins to ponder the possibility of earlier retirement. It does not dawn on him that the problem may be in the inner world, in the way he relates to what he does. In American culture the bias is always that the outer situation is at fault. Changing the environment is the key. So when Remen suggests inner work that will take valuable time, he initially resists.

This cultural bias is operative in most of us. If we want to enrich our lives and recover passion and purpose in what we do, our instincts will push us toward new relationships and new environments. We might hear the suggestion of a spiritual practice that works with new mental categories as indirect, time-consuming, and too "iffy." What exactly will it accomplish?

With a little humor ("Less expensive than Prozac"), Rachel urges him to give it a try. He goes along and begins the practice. Often transformative spiritual practices are foreign territory and not particularly appealing. We may have to trust a teacher/counselor/friend who has more experience and will accompany us. It is never quite clear what gets people to "take this leap," and if the resistance is absolute, nothing happens. Just to begin a spiritual practice, we may have to overcome cultural ideas about what counts as important and what is a good use of our time.

Gradualness

In the surgeon's eyes, the practice is not an immediate success. He sees nothing that surprises, inspires, or moves him. But his ego, "I don't like to fail at things," along with Rachel's guidance moves him forward. He begins to notice surface surprises, but hardly anything that would move or inspire him. But then "something happens." His perception is beginning to shift. As he listens to his patients, he discerns their underlying spirit and from this awakening moves on to a new interpersonal style. "He began to ask other people one or two questions that he had not been taught to ask in medical school. 'What has sustained you in dealing with this illness?' or 'Where do you find your strength?' . . . What they said was true for him, too, as he struggled to deal with the difficulties of his own life." Reciprocity, a sharing of life deeper than social roles, is a tip-off the spiritual dimension has been engaged.

Although there may be significant breakthroughs while engaging in a spiritual practice, new perceptions do not happen all at once. There is often sequencing. We see nothing, and we have to dwell in darkness. Then we see a light that, in turn, dissolves into a greater light. Insights give way to further insights. In other words, a spiritual practice entails standing still and moving, standing still and moving. It is often difficult to be comfortable with both positions. But gradualness is how many people experience growth in a transformative spiritual practice. The advice of spiritual traditions should be heeded.

"Act upon the little light you have, and more will be given. Resist such action because the light is so dim and because you want more certainty in advance, and the light will grow still dimmer."[3]

Integration

For the surgeon, what happens during practice time does not easily carry over into daytime, into the rest of life. He can see clearly at night when he is reviewing his day through his new eyes. He has twenty-twenty vision when looking through the rearview mirror. But, while it is happening, he is missing in action. Insights and realizations that happen during practice time are forgotten in the midst of the fray of living. This is typical.

Although this initial disjunction between practice time and daytime is partial, it is not negative. The surgeon evaluates it positively: "I was building up a capacity I had never used. But I got better at it. Once I began to see things at the time they actually happened, a lot changed for me." Integrating the spiritual truths seen so clearly in practice time into work and relationships is a piecemeal and ongoing effort. However, the goal is action, and eventually the surgeon is able to say what he sees. When he does this, his life and the lives of his patients change. The movement is from inner to outer, from a change of mind to a change of behavior.

"Turning the Wheel": A Traditional Story of a Transformative Spiritual Practice

Three men lived along a caravan route in the desert. They made their living buying and selling trinkets and goods from the caravan passengers. They made a very good living and were considered excellent merchants.

However, this is not what they dreamed about. They dreamed of being gardeners. But how could they be gardeners in a desert? How could they make something grow in a deserted place?

Then they heard the master gardener would be coming through on the next caravan. They decided to invite him to teach them the art of gardening. The master gardener heard about these aspiring gardeners. So when his caravan arrived, he decided to visit them.

He arrived at the house of the first man and, upon entering, asked him, "Do you want to grow something in this deserted place?" The man knew this question would be asked and he had given it considerable thought. He realized that he liked to daydream about gardening, talk to his friends about gardening, even read books about gardening. But when it came right down to it, he did not really want to be a gardener. He had little or no desire to make something grow in a deserted place. So he told the master gardener, "No."

The master gardener smiled and said, "Fine. Now is not the time." Then he left and proceeded to the home of the second man.

Upon entering the house of the second man, the master gardener asked, "Do you want to make something grow in this deserted place?" The man had given this question serious thought and he had projected where it would lead. It would begin with a conversation between himself and the master gardener. The conversation would start with the practicalities of the gardening—how to open the earth, how to plant the seed, how to close the earth, how and when to water it, what to do when it began to grow. Then they would soar from these practicalities to philosophy and talk about gardening as a way of life, how its wisdom would apply to families, government, education, health care. This conversation would grow so rich and full that it would conclude with a prayer to the One Who Makes All Things Grow. This is what the second man thought, and this is what he expected.

So when the master gardener asked, "Do you want to grow something in this deserted place?" the man replied, "Yes," and was about to go further when the master gardener held up his hand and simply said, "Wait here. I will be back."

The master gardener returned two days later and said, "There is a wheel in the back of the plot of land that will be the site of your future garden. Turn it one full turn every afternoon." Then the master gardener left.

The man was disappointed. This is not what he had expected. He went to the site of his future garden and saw the wheel. He turned it one full turn. He did the same the second and third days. However, the fourth and fifth days he had business elsewhere. The sixth day he turned it. The seventh day he forgot. So it continued; some days he turned the wheel and some days he did not. After two months his neighbors arrived, saw nothing had grown in his garden, and asked him why. He told them flatly, "The master gardener is a sham. If you want to grow something, do not ask him."

Meanwhile, the master gardener had arrived at the home of the third man. Upon entering, he asked him, "Do you want to grow something in this deserted place?" The man said he did, and the master gardener told him to wait and he would return. Two days later he returned and said, "There is a wheel in the back of your future garden. Turn it one full turn every afternoon."

What the man did not know was the master gardener had installed an underground irrigation system. With each turn of the wheel it released hidden waters deep in the earth that only gradually would reach and nourish the surface.

The third man was also disappointed by these terse instructions, but he followed them faithfully. Then one day something happened that disturbed him greatly. Something began to grow. Green shoots shot up through the cracked and parched earth. At the sight of the green growth the man became anxious. How would he keep the plants alive and flourishing? The master gardener had given him no detailed plan. The man was beside himself with worry.

Then he made a remarkable discovery. Instead of worrying about how to keep the green growth alive, he looked at the plants themselves. On each leaf were instructions about what to do next. The man followed the instructions and soon his home was surrounded by a lovely garden. The neighbors came and exclaimed, "How did you ever grow this beautiful garden in this deserted place?" The man shrugged and said, "It seemed to happen naturally. I persevered and tried not to have too many expectations."

Four Challenges from "Turning the Wheel"

Desire

In this story three men cultivate a dream about gardening. When the master gardener arrives, he pressures this dream toward reality by explicitly asking, "Do you want to grow something in this deserted place?" For the first man the dream has not deepened into desire. It is a mere wish, and not a passionate commitment. The teacher moves on. Desire is critical. Without desire, the first man is not ready and the teacher is not needed.

But what exactly is the desire that the first man lacks and the other two men have? Symbolically stated, it is the desire to grow something in a place where nothing grows. They do not want to grow something in a valley of rich soil, but in the hard and crusted desert where nothing takes root. They want fruitfulness to occur in a place that cannot produce fruit on its own.

This is similar to another desire in biblical and spiritual literature. Abraham and Sarah and Zachary and Elizabeth want a child, but they are beyond childbearing years. They want fruitfulness to occur in a place (the womb) that cannot produce fruit (a child) on its own. Therefore, if the garden grows and the child is conceived, this ancient spiritual mindset concludes that God must have been present because the natural elements do not have the potential to produce the fruit. We may water, as St. Paul suggested, but God gives growth (1 Cor 3:6). Or as Ezekiel put it, when the Messiah comes, the desert will bloom (Isa 35:2). It takes the coming of the Messiah because the desert does not have blooming potential of its own. It has to be visited and infused by a power of fruitfulness.

The two men desire to produce fruit in unlikely places by bringing to those places the presence of God. They want to become fruitful with the help of God. This desire is the necessary background to engage in the practice. Without this desire the master gardener does not propose the practice. This desire is not just a first step. It is the permeating context of all that follows. This desire will be revisited every time there is difficulty in the practice and every time a reason must be given for why the practice is being pursued. The practice does not happen in a vacuum. The practice is the way the desire is pursued.

Expectations

The second man not only has the desire but also a set of expectations. He knows exactly how the master gardener should teach him and what the results should be. As he contemplates this imagined scenario, he creates the conditions of his own formation. He will become a desert gardener on his own terms. However, the master gardener has another way. He is not a talkative man, and he does not supply information and secrets that can be used. Rather he creates the conditions through which a person can realize his or her own desire.

The instructions are simple. The second man is told to turn a wheel; in the turning he will learn. However, this practice does not fit into his imagined scenario. He turns the wheel reluctantly and haphazardly. Nothing grows, and he blames the inadequate teaching of the master gardener. The teacher becomes the scapegoat.

When expectations are held too tightly, they deceive us into thinking we can know before we know. The mind is always comparing what is happening to what it thinks should be happening. This mental activity leads to smugness when things turn out as we imagined and disappointment when they do not. So we find ourselves vacillating between arrogance and disgruntlement. The story suggests we learn the skill of refraining from predictions, refusing to let the fierce, ordering drive of the mind race ahead. This ability to bracket expectations is often called a negative capability, the refusal to let the mind create and subscribe to scenarios without the benefit of actual experience. It is in the same category as T. S. Eliot's advice to "wait without hope / For hope would be hope for the wrong thing."[4] In other words, the wheel has to be turned with persevering attention.

Perseverance

Transformative spiritual practices come with instructions, usually about when and how to do them. In this story the master gardener has the men turn the wheel, one full turn, every afternoon. Often the instructions are deceptively simple. OK, one full turn every afternoon. But after the practice is actually engaged, the wisdom of the instructions become more evident. For some reason it is one full turn and not a half or three-quarter turn. Also, it has to happen in the afternoon.

Morning and evening are not the proper times. The story itself does not tell us the precise meaning of these instructions. Its major point is more direct: if the garden dreamers are not faithful to these instructions, nothing will grow. Perseverance is essential.

The second gardener has very good excuses—business elsewhere, forgetfulness, a submerged resentment that his expectations are not guiding the process, and so forth. All this is expected. Taking up a transformative spiritual practice always happens in the midst of a life filled with other demands and responsibilities. If it becomes one more thing and enters into competition for a busy person's time and attention, its value will come under scrutiny and it just may lose its priority.

The third character reveals an important feature of transformative spiritual practices. Although he does not know exactly why these instructions have been given, he turns the wheel every day. He stays with the actions he has been told to do. He perseveres without full knowledge. Quite simply, there is a need to trust the process, although all of the process is not known. This is a standard point of view: you do not have to trust the teacher completely and forever, but you have to trust the teacher initially until you come to know for yourself.

Attention

In spiritual teaching stories the readers/listeners are the ones who are ultimately being taught. So although the third character does not know all that is entailed in turning the wheel, the storyteller provides the readers/listeners with the full picture. In his two-day absence from the third garden dreamer, the master gardener has installed an underground irrigation system. The wheel is connected to a secret flow of water in the deep darkness of the earth. The faithful turning of the wheel is releasing waters beneath the surface that will eventually bear fruit above the surface. The growth begins in hiddenness; it is unseen. Important and needed work is happening beneath the level of consciousness that will eventually enter into consciousness.

The symbol of the green shoots breaking through the encrusted desert floor means a change in consciousness has begun to surface. However, instead of it being eagerly accepted, it causes anxiety. What does this growth mean and how is it nurtured? The master gardener has given no instructions, so the third man is "on his own." However, there are instructions, but they are not where he is looking. When he stops worrying about where it is going and starts paying attention to what is growing, he finds the instructions about what to do next are written on the leaves.

The change of consciousness he has undergone as he turned the wheel suggests its own way forward. When he follows those instructions, the garden grows even more extensively and surrounds his house. His confession to his neighbors makes the point. This wonder has happened because he persevered and tried not to have too many expectations. In other words, he paid attention to what was happening and heeded what it told him. He learned to notice and participate in his own experience of transformative spiritual growth.

Teacher/Director

Besides the practice itself and what the one practicing may encounter, there is the important role of the teacher/director. In "Finding New Eyes" Rachel Remen functions as a combination of counselor/spiritual director. She suggests the actual exercise and, as he practices, suggests changes in his attitude toward what he is doing. She also has ongoing conversations with him and helps him finds the language to articulate the changes in his interpersonal style that is giving him increased meaning and satisfaction. Although what the surgeon is becoming aware of is how the spirit suffuses physical, psychological, and social reality bringing wholeness into relationships, spirit is not mentioned. The practice is carried out and commented on in secular language. This is often the comfort level of contemporary transformative practices.

In "Turning the Wheel" the master gardener is a classic spiritual teacher. He seeks out those who dream of gardening, determines the presence or absence of their desire, and sets up the conditions for their dream to become reality. As is often the case in ancient traditions, he does not lecture them with his wisdom but creatively designs conditions that will bring them to the necessary spiritual knowledge on their own. Once he has set the conditions and given the instructions, he disappears. The third gardener has to solve his dilemma—what to do when something starts growing—on his own. In this story the role of the teacher/director is in the setup and not in the accompaniment.

Spiritual teachers/directors are needed for those who undertake transformative spiritual practices. What exactly their role will be can never be completely spelled out. Often in contemporary culture a combination of skills in counseling and traditional spiritual direction seem appropriate. But, from my point of view, what is a requirement is their personal experience with the practice they are suggesting and supervising. Furthermore, a speculative and practical knowledge of how the community has valued and used this practice is extremely helpful.

This puts the teacher/director a little further down the road. He or she knows some of the smoothness and roughness and can communicate to those practicing a comforting and crucial perspective—they are not the first and they are not alone. When this is done, the important dimension of community is brought into the experience. We are in a community of humans who have tried to spiritually develop through this practice. Belonging to this community is a source of resiliency and perseverance.

Conclusion

Our concern is with praying the Our Father. But this particular practice is a species of the wider genus of transformative spiritual practices. So most likely we will have to work with some of the seven challenges of this genus. We will

- discover resistance in ourselves and in our situations,
- be impatient with gradualness but have to submit to it,
- puzzle how this practice is influencing our interpersonal and social life,
- revisit our fundamental desire in order to continue the practice,
- deal with our expectations that insist our experience be different than it actually is,
- develop the perseverance to do the practice each day,
- pay careful attention to what is happening to us as we receive the instructions about what to do next.

Through it all, it will be helpful if an experienced spiritual teacher/director is walking with us.

Of course, these challenges will be individualized, applying to each of us in particularized ways. How large they will loom and how we will respond to them will be related to our personal histories and tolerances. But the recommended approach is not to let these challenges become problems to be solved, stumbling blocks that confuse the mind and threaten the continuance of the practice. They should be engaged as adaptive challenges, an ongoing part of the work we have decided to do. They are opportunities that help us move into the awakened consciousness of the realities the words of the Our Father are meant to express and communicate. They are not obstacles; they are part of the path.

CHAPTER 3

Seven Challenges of Praying the Our Father

The seven challenges of transformative spiritual practices in general illumine the experience of praying the Our Father. Most likely, all seven will come into play if our practice is taken seriously and persevered in for a long period of time (over a year). But, first and foremost, praying the Our Father is a particular practice of the Christian tradition. As such, it has its own set challenges that must be engaged.

These challenges come from the language and structure of the prayer itself. But the language and structure of the prayer is indebted to the Bible as a whole and to the gospels in particular. So the challenges reflect those larger contexts and are only fully understood within them. Furthermore, the prayer has traveled with Christians through time and space, and the journey has naturally brought struggle and adaptation. The Christian tradition, especially the spiritual, liturgical, and ethical traditions, has contributed insights and refinements about how to pray the Our Father. Finally, challenges arise from the interaction of the prayer with contemporary sensibilities. We engage the prayer out of our personal histories and cultural conditioning, and that means we bring hesitancies and enthusiasms to our practice. All of this is present when we pray, sometimes implicitly and sometimes explicitly.

However, no matter where the challenges come from, identifying them serves the same agenda as describing the seven challenges of transformative spiritual practices in general. In fact, some of the distinctive Christian challenges overlap with the general challenges. They alert us both to what we will encounter and what we will need to resolve in order to move forward. Even if challenges are set aside for good or bad reasons, the odds are eventually they will have to be met. Therefore, this chapter will identify and develop seven challenges that most likely will emerge as we engage the practice of praying the Our Father:

- Putting on the mind of Christ
- Translating symbols into meanings
- Connecting religious motivation and social action
- Petitioning as a way of opening
- Holding together faith, understanding, and realization
- Integrating into the day
- Syncing mind and mouth

Reflection on these areas is more than just remote preparation for praying. It will shape the content and process of the actual prayer experience.

Putting on the Mind of Christ

Catholic Christianity has a reputation as a creedal religion. The Apostles' Creed informs catechetical approaches and the Nicene Creed occupies the bridge space in the Mass between the Liturgy of the Word and the Liturgy of the Eucharist. Also, a long history of councils has wrestled with disputes about what to believe and produced dogmatic statements with the status of "defined faith" that theologians have pondered and elaborated. Therefore, people entering into the Catholic faith and seeking to grow in it immediately meet creeds and dogmas. These provide the standard answers to the question, "What do you believe?"

However, beneath this creedal emphasis there is another complementary tradition. Catholic Christianity has always been what it was called in the beginning, "the Way." It is a following of Jesus, an imitation of Christ. This is the path of participating in Word and sacrament as well as meditating on gospel texts. Praying the Our Father is a key practice of this imitation of Christ. Therefore, if there is a desire for faith development, the way forward is to learn to pray the Our Father so that it informs consciousness and structures perceptions that lead to actions. The question of this tradition of following Jesus is not "What do you believe?" but "What is your practice?"

Our practice is praying the Our Father.

As an introduction to the kenosis prayer/hymn in Philippians, Paul enjoins his readers, "Let the same mind be in you that was in Christ Jesus" (Phil 2:5, NRSV). This "same mind" injunction could be used to introduce the practice of praying the Our Father. It is assumed there is a structure of consciousness (a mind) in the prayer that is indebted to Jesus and is able to be transferred to his followers. It is embedded in the words and phrases of the prayer; and if we apprentice ourselves to those words and phrases they will awaken us to the spiritual realities that energized Jesus. The mind of the prayer will become our mind.

This focus on "mind" is important because mind is the gatekeeper of spirit. Philip Novak spells out this connection between mind and spirit in terms of the locus and the goal of spiritual disciplines:

> When speaking of "spiritual disciplines" it is helpful to re-member that the word "spiritual" points to the *goal* of the work and not to its actual *locus* [italics mine]. For it is not the spirit that needs discipline. "Spirit" or its equivalent in other traditions points to the unconditioned dimension of ourselves which dwells in a timeless union with the Real and which is to be discovered or uncovered by means of the disciplines.
>
> The true *locus* of the spiritual discipline . . . is the psyche, that interdependent network of conditioned structures which forms and informs our very states of consciousness, our identities and our varying notions of what counts as valuable and real. . . . Consciousness and the structures which determine it thus comprise the pivot point between whomever we think we are and ultimate reality. [Spiritual] discipline aims at nothing less than the transformation of the undergirding structures of our con-sciousness . . . both for our own welfare and for that of the human community.[1]

Praying the Our Father is a spiritual practice and so shares in the ambition of spiritual disciplines. Its agenda is to change "the structures of consciousness that . . . comprise the pivot point between whomever we think we are and ultimate real-ity." The assumption is the mind of the prayer has the capacity to do this in the minds of the ones praying. If the two come together, Spirit will be released for the good of the ones pray-ing and the good of the human community.

This distinction between the locus and goal of a spiritual practice interprets a common experience. We say our prayers, but nothing happens in us. We persevere out of habit and/or obligation. However, a long stretch of this praying without any illumination of the mind, inspiration of the will, or glad-dening of the heart—in other words without any touch of Spirit—makes us weary. It is often difficult to diagnose the problem. But this distinction suggests the mind of the prayer and the mind of the ones praying might not be in enough sync to release Spirit. Therefore, the challenge is to concentrate on the mind of the prayer and how it is transferring to the mind of the ones praying. Spirit waits, but is the mind open?

Translating Symbols into Meanings

Making the mind of the prayer our mind is not easy. One reason for this is the language of the prayer is largely symbolic, and we have a tendency to take it literally. If the Gospel of John is any indication, this literal penchant is deeply entrenched in our human makeup. Nicodemus takes Jesus' remark about being born again as an instruction to return to his mother's womb (John 3:4). The Samaritan woman thinks living water comes from a well dug in the earth and can be drawn up with a bucket (John 4:12). Peter takes Jesus' insistence to wash his feet as a podiatrist might and extends it into a complete bath-ing event of hands and head as well (John 13:10). Both the disciples and the authorities find Jesus' words that he is "the living bread that came down from heaven" and they have to "eat the flesh of the Son of Man and drink his blood" a hard saying, that is, perplexing (John 6:51, 53, 60). This literalism keeps the characters from changing their minds and opening to the reality of Spirit that the language is meant to release.

Yet this literal knee-jerk response to symbolic language is understandable. We talk about the spiritual dimension of life in images taken from the physical, psychological, social, and cosmic dimensions; and there is good reason for this. The spiritual permeates these dimensions and elevates them to their maximum potential. So they are natural candidates to express and communicate Spirit. In gospel language, it is "earthly" language in service of "heavenly reality." However, when we hear or read these images, we tend to take them on their own terms—as statements about their own dimensions and not as statements about Spirit. After all, we are most comfortable in talking directly about physical, psychological, social, and cosmic dynamics. We do this every day. In fact, we have appropriate languages for each dimension and the various operations within that dimension. So naturally when we hear these languages, those habits kick in and we are down familiar paths before we know it. Therefore, to deal with symbolic language, we must consciously make an effort to stop the automatic tendencies of the literal mind.

But more than that is necessary to uncover the mind of the prayer. The prayer is a series of succinct symbols. It is like a Christian elevator speech. It insinuates a lot with a little. To anyone familiar with the Hebrew (Old Testament) and Greek (New Testament) Scriptures, the words of the Our Father are springboards. "Father," "heaven and earth," "name," "will," "kingdom," "bread," "forgiveness," "temptation," and "evil" deeply resonate and allude to many other biblical passages. The *Catechism of the Catholic Church* (2761–72) recognizes this succinctness of the Lord's Prayer and evaluates it, following Tertullian and other Christian thinkers, as a summary of the whole gospel.

This is high praise, but it may be overpraise. Although the phrases can imitate the overture to a symphony and suggest in miniature the larger renditions to come, they can also lose their precision and punch in this function. The Our Father is not everything, but it is quite definitely something. The gospels, the New Testament, and indeed the entire Bible cover vast territories and beneath these inspired witnesses are uncharted human and cosmic experiences. The prayer could get lost in these expanses. So while its succinctness needs development, we must be careful not to thin it out so its flow loses its impact—its radical articulation of human identity and mission.

Christians have always been challenged by the compactness of the phrases of the Our Father. Almost everyone appreciates more is going on beneath the surface of the words. There is an intuition of an excess of meaning that should be developed in order to pray the prayer authentically. To respond to this faith instinct, sometimes paraphrases would be created, strings of words that stayed in the prayer mode and developed the image. "O My Father, tender in love, tender in thy care and providence over me, all-sufficient in thy power and provisions for me, and so to everyone, and the more so by being so unto us all."[2] Other times there might be a quick, almost bullet-point type of assistance. "Hallowed be Thy Name: selfless adoration, awestruck worship as the ruling temper of our life and all we do."[3] At other times, longer expositions would be developed. These would be read or preached before and perhaps after the actual praying. These expositions informed the minds and hearts of the ones praying at the same time as it gave them considerable latitude about what thoughts and feelings they might bring to the actual words. But the bottom line of any approach is this: the average person praying the Our Father needs and, most likely, welcomes interpretive help.

Therefore, the allusive power of the phrases makes the prayer a train. Once we are on board, the evocative images carry us into a world of associated stories, especially gospel stories. Once these stories are consulted, we begin to grasp the extended meanings of the images and express them in ideas, especially in ideas that are relevant to contemporary sensibilities. Once the images and stories enter into the stream of ideas, they accumulate more and more meanings. So when we pray the prayer in a reflective way, inevitably we go down an interpretive path. Images, stories, and ideas unfold naturally and combine to provide a rich and varied feast of accompanying language. Choosing from this abundant menu to create a nourishing meal is the task at hand.

Bede Griffiths provides an example of creating an accompanying language to a prayer practice.[4] His practice is the Jesus Prayer of the Russian pilgrim—"Lord Jesus Christ, Son of God, have mercy on me, a sinner." Each phrase shapes his mental awareness in a certain way. When he says Lord Jesus Christ, he considers Jesus as the Word "that enlightens everyone coming into the world, and though they may not recognize it, is present in every human being in the depth of their soul." When he says "have mercy on me, a sinner," he unites himself "with all human beings from the beginning of the world who have experienced separation from God, or from eternal truth." Under the guidance of the prayer he becomes conscious of both divine presence and our absence from it. This consciously appropriated Jesus Prayer shapes his awareness. It directs his mind toward the spiritual dimensions of the self and the world and their need to come together in wholeness.

What Griffiths has done over the years is develop an interpretive complementary language for the concise and condensed words of the prayer. Therefore, when he says the prayer—either interiorly or out loud, either alone or with others—he prays the words of the prayer while his mind follows the developed meanings. Although he does not tell us, my guess is that these meanings took shape over a number of years under the influence of study, prayer, and experience. They probably do not have a "set language," but they have what might be called a baseline set of meanings. The set language is the prayer formula itself: "Lord Jesus Christ, Son of God, have mercy on me, a sinner." The accompanying language shifts and develops, but basically builds on established meanings. Therefore, the prayer grows in meanings as the one who prays it grows in spiritual perception and action.

This same type of development needs to be done with those who pray the Our Father. The Our Father is a series of words created and handed on by people who were in touch with the interior truth these words signify. As we pray the prayer, we too can come into inner correspondence with the spiritual realities the words express and communicate. As that happens and in order for that to happen on a regular basis, we need to develop interpretations, meanings that help the mind focus and sustain its path of change. The words of the prayer do not change; they are the "set language." However, over the years the accompanying meanings develop and the language shifts.

Connecting Religious Motivation and Social Action

A significant feature of those meanings and how they are structured within the prayer is that they are both religious and social. More specifically, they are about how religious meaning motivates and informs social action. To be a son and daughter of God (religious meaning) is to embody the "values" of God in social situations (social action). As some say, the vertical relationship to God translates into the horizontal relationship to the people and events of the world. This is the central dynamic of the first half of the prayer, bringing heaven to earth. The gospels assume this connection between religious meaning and social action. Even more, they assume humans have an innate desire to enter into this relationship and cooperate with its energies. In other words, the religious meaning becomes the sustaining motivation for social action.

Although this connection of religious meaning/motivation and social action is central to the gospel and the Lord's Prayer, it is a difficult connection for our secular consciousness to "get into." At first glance this does not seem to be the case. We engage in extensive meaning-making activity, situating parts into larger wholes. When we trace bodily symptoms to causes, we gain physical meaning. When we find the deeper reasoning and energy of an aberrant idea or feeling, we create psychological meaning. When we tie a particular occurrence to larger causes and contexts, social meaning emerges. Cosmic meaning happens when incidents of the earth are connected to larger patterns of the universe. Religious meaning happens when individual people and events are seen from an ultimate perspective, from the relationship to the final reality that permeates and transcends the physical, psychological, social, and cosmic. Therefore, we generate meanings across a spectrum of human dimensions—physical, psychological, social, cosmic, religious.

We also seem to be engaged in this meaning-making activity all the time, finding larger contexts for everything about us. This is why Ken Wilber often observes that men and women are "condemned to meaning."[5] Meanings in the physical, psychological, social, and cosmic dimensions come about through reflection on ordinary experience and through knowledge made available from professionals who study these dimensions—the full and complex variety of scientists. We seem to gravitate naturally toward participating in and creating these meanings. And we know their importance. Robert Emmons observes about social meaning, "Embedding one's finite life within a grander, all-encompassing narrative appears to be a universal human need, and the inability to do so leads to despair and self destructive behavior."[6] Meanings do not seem to be optional, and they are intrinsically related to our overall well-being.

However, as strong as this drive to meaning is, it can be resisted. We can cultivate a "negative capability," allowing things to be on their own, refusing them context and perspective. This is particularly true in the realm of religious meaning. Religious meaning places individual finite life in the context of ultimate reality, a reality that transcends and yet permeates physical, psychological, social, and cosmic dimensions. As such, it often seems more esoteric and not as easily available. To our secular sensibilities, constructing and espousing religious meaning seems a precarious undertaking and one that it is difficult to be certain about and on which to stake our commitments and behaviors. Since the Our Father is about religious meaning and its social ramifications, it has to dialogue with these hesitancies.

Ken Wilber has pointed out this refusal to entertain religious meaning:

> The wonders of creation—who needs a source for them? The bigness of creation!—who could ask for more? Let me bask in the riches of the sensory world, and reason upon it where necessary, but why ask behind the scenes for more than this display? Let cosmic emotion and piety carry the day, and let me weep with joy at any passing sight in nature that strikes the slightest chord of egoic sentiment, and let me spend my days and nights suckling shadows that are dear enough to me. And let me never, never, never sin by asking beyond the shaded nooks and crannies. Let me always be known for saving and defending the wonderful appearances, and with eyes so modestly reverted from the all-embracing Source.[7]

Although there may be strong attachments to physical, psychological, social, and cosmic meanings, there may be what the gospels call a "slow heart" when it comes to taking the step toward ultimacy. Our eyes, as Wilber points out, are "modestly reverted from the all-embracing Source."

One response to this avoidance of religious meaning as the motivating source of social action is to reassert how essential it is to a full and authentic human life. Kathleen Brehony recalled Carl Jung's insistence on the importance of religious meaning:

> Carl Jung believed that there is only one decisive question that human beings need ask, and that is, Am I related to something infinite or not? "That is," he wrote, "the telling question of life. Only if we know that the thing that truly matters is the infinite can we avoid fixing our attention upon futilities and upon all kinds of goals, which are not of real importance. . . . In the final analysis, we count for something only because of the essential we embody, and if we do not embody that, life is wasted."[8]

This idea that "life is wasted" if it is not connected to God is also reflected in Alfred North Whitehead's often quoted remark, "Apart from God every activity is a passing whiff of insignificance." Even in our most down moments, most of us would like to avoid being "a passing whiff of insignificance." So while we may vacillate about attempts to ground intrapersonal, interpersonal, and social dynamics in a religious meaning that has motivational impact, we also discover in ourselves a hunger that only religious meaning can satisfy.

Petitioning as a Way of Opening

The Our Father has a reputation for being a prayer of petition. In fact, there have been ongoing debates whether the prayer contains six or seven petitions. But on closer look, the language of the prayer is more complex. What are often considered the first three petitions—"hallowed be thy name. / Thy kingdom come. / Thy will be done"—may not be directly asking the heavenly Father to bring about these realities on earth.[9] Rather the ones praying are aligning themselves with the agenda of the heavenly Father. It is not the language of asking; it is the language of shared commitment. However, the last four phrases explicitly employ petition language; and, in doing so, they may tap into some mental conditioning that is very hard to avoid.

We are all familiar with the experience of asking someone for something. Of course, it is extremely important who that someone is and what that something is we are requesting. But if that someone is important and that something is connected to our survival or the quality of our life, a protocol kicks in. We may find ourselves begging from powerful people who have access to what we need. This may include praising them excessively to the point of flattery and pleading with them profusely to the point of humiliation. But we are desperate, and desperate people do what they have to.

It is easy to transport this begging/survival scenario and its strategies into prayer situations. We have all experienced helplessness, situations where all the human resources we can get our hands on cannot bring about the results we want. It is natural to scream at the sky one moment and to beg from the beyond in the next moment. Finitude makes us vulnerable and fuels the way we ask. Our anxious petitioning might be such a strong mental conditioning that it becomes the dominant way we pray. It may be the first way we pray; and maybe it is the only way we pray. Perhaps this is why some claim all prayer comes down to one word, "Help!" This form of petitioning is deeply ingrained, and it will not be relativized or replaced easily. We may find ourselves bringing it, wittingly or unwittingly, into praying the Lord's Prayer.

However, this type of petitioning may not be the consciousness the prayer wants to generate. In fact, as we saw in chapter 2, criticisms of petitioning surround the text of the

Lord's Prayer in the Gospel of Matthew. Jesus introduces *his* prayer with, "When you are praying, do not heap up empty phrases as the Gentiles do; for they think that they will be heard because of their many words. Do not be like them, for your Father knows what you need before you ask him" (Matt 6:7-8, NRSV). The supposition is that the phrases of the Our Father are not "heaped up" but carefully chosen; they are not "empty" but meaningful and strategic. There are not a lot of them because praying is not an attempt to persuade a reluctant God. It is not a matter of "storming heaven." In fact, physical and social needs do not have to be presented because they are already known by the One to whom the prayer is addressed. Is the assumption that asking for needs is not necessary when you are dealing with God under the image "heavenly Father" because God is already responding to them?

The Lukan Jesus also has some wisdom about petitioning and how it relates to praying the Lord's Prayer.[10] After Jesus tells his disciples the shortened form of the Lord's Prayer, he engages in a complex and imaginative argument that is meant to give them the courage and confidence to ask, seek, and knock (Luke 11:1-13). He tells his disciples two stories. In the first story, a friend who is not disposed to give out of friendship eventually gives food out of the fear of being shamed. In the second story, parents, who are characterized as evil, give good things (an egg and a fish) rather than deceptive substitutes (a scorpion and a snake) to their children. In both stories giving goes on in the human community, even though the ones giving are not completely and rightly disposed to give.

The key to both stories is the conclusion Jesus draws: "*how much more* will the Father in heaven give the holy Spirit to those who ask him?" (Luke 11:13, emphasis added). This is a classic style of argument. If giving happens in the human community with all its counter-forces, complexities, and ambiguities, how much more will it go on when none of these are present and the nature of the heavenly Father is to give the Holy Spirit? So it is not valid not to ask because we fear the One we ask may be conflicted and reluctant to give and we will have to go through the abasement of begging. Instead we should embrace the injunctions that connect the two stories. "[A]sk and you will receive; seek and you will find; knock and the door will be opened to you. For everyone who asks, receives; and the one who seeks, finds; and to the one who knocks, the door will be opened" (Luke 11:9-10). The confidence of success spurs the petitioning.

What is the wisdom of the Matthean and Lukan Jesus about how to pray the Our Father? The "heavenly Father" is a self-giving power of love into the ones who can open to this reality. So there is no need to petition God imaged as "heavenly Father" as if this reality was not already engaged and active in human life. The essence of "heavenly Father" is the pouring out of Spirit. But this activity has to be discerned and cooperated with. Since it is already present and not absent, the question is how to become aware of it and cooperate with it. The images of "asking, seeking, and knocking" articulate our effort to enter into the spiritual dynamics of the "heavenly Father." This is the energy we bring to praying the Lord's Prayer, the energy of discernment and alignment. We are not asking God as imaged as the "heavenly Father" to intervene and do something. We are trying to get on board with what the love of the self-giving God is already doing.

But why employ petitioning language? Why say, "Give us . . . Forgive us . . . Lead us . . . Deliver us?" If it is not functioning in a literal way, how is it functioning?

First, it stresses grace, the priority of divine agency. From a religious point of view, human actors are always in a responding mode; they are either cooperating with or resisting the grace that is coming from the immanent-transcendent Mystery. The major images for our relationship to God—creature, child, and servant—carry this "firstness of God" consciousness. These images presuppose a larger and more important reality that defines our identities. The creature lives by the energies of the creator; the servant is about the work of the master; the child embodies the parents. The petitioning structure of the prayer acknowledges this situation. This reality pre-exists our appearance and will post-exist our departure. However we want to think about ourselves, religious sensibilities suggest we move in the directions of dependency on something larger and service to its agenda. It is built into our finitude. As Paul says simply, "[We] are not [our] own" (1 Cor 6:19).

Second, asking language, especially when seeking and knocking language accompanies it, emphasizes our openness, our readiness for awareness and engagement. This is what we will be looking for. The kingdom is at risk in all the situations that "bread" symbolizes, in the interpersonal dynamics of forgiveness, and when the temptations to do evil pull at our freedom. With the petitioning consciousness we are awake to the spiritual lures in these areas and the creative paths they are opening. When petitioning does not focus on waiting for the response of the One being asked but on the heightened attention of the one asking, then praying the Lord's Prayer is first and foremost what it is designed to be—the *metanoia* (change of mind) that opens and responds to the movement of God.

Third, the question of whether petitioning God is asking for and expecting God to intervene as a separate agent of activity can be bracketed. The God emphasis throughout the prayer has another function. Asking for God's name, kingdom, and will; and for God to give bread, participate in the dynamics of forgiveness, and keep us from temptation and evil is a critique of how the world is presently handling these crucial affairs.

We are asking that earth become like heaven because earth has become intolerable. God's way must replace the present way humans conduct business.

Underlying petitioning is a sense of profound dissatisfaction and lament. We have abandoned the biblical demands for distributive and restorative justice that should characterize social life.[11] The Creator did not intend the earth to be this way; and since Jesus is a Jew of the first commandment who has no other gods before Yahweh the Liberator of the oppressed, things must change. In its earliest context, the petitioning of God in the Lord's Prayer can be read as a howl of discontent.

Holding Together Faith, Understanding, and Realization

I learned the Our Father from my parents (my mother was the primary teacher) and the Sisters of Mercy in St. Catherine of Sienna parochial school. It was a faith inheritance, passed on to me as it was passed on to my parents and the Sisters of Mercy. This prayer piece of the faith, the Our Father, connected me to Jesus. It originated in the community of the Gospel of St. Matthew. But since then, millennia of people had prayed it. So it also positioned me in the lineup of all the people who passed on the prayer from Jesus to me. As I taught the prayer to others, I moved from one of the more recent recipients to a more middle link in the chain; but I was still in the chain. I belonged to the Catholic community and a tradition through saying and sharing this prayer.[12]

In my practice of praying the Our Father, sometimes I remember this dynamic of faith transmission. I like the feeling of being part of a long historical process, of stretching backward into the past and forward into the future. I also like the feeling of being handed something precious, something worthwhile that others thought would hold me in good stead. "Passing on" from generation to generation somewhat counters the lostness for which time is so famous. In fact, part of what I bring to mind as I begin the prayer with "Our" is all the people who have prayed it and passed it on. It bonds my individual finite self to the individual finite selves of those who have come before me and those who will come after me.

But belonging to the people of the prayer implies more than just the brute fact of transmission. It also means entering into a history of practice and interpretation of the prayer, dialoguing with spiritually developed people whose consciousness is more fully aligned with the prayer than mine will ever be. Borrowing from their experience because they have been "closer to the fire" is a natural way we gain confidence in the convictions of the prayer. Charles Taylor underlines this experience of community and tradition:

> It goes without saying that for most people who undergo a conversion there may never have been one of those seemingly self-authenticating experiences . . . but they may easily take on a new view about religion from others: saints, prophets, charismatic leaders, who have radiated some sense of more direct contact.
>
> This sense that others have been closer is an essential part of the ordinary person's confidence in a shared religious language, or a way of articulating fullness. These may be named figures, identified paradigms, like Francis of Assisi, or Saint Teresa; or Jonathan Edwards, or John Wesley; or they may figure as the unnamed company of (to oneself) unknown saints or holy people. In either case (and often these two are combined), the language one adheres to is given force by the conviction that others have lived it in a more complete, direct and powerful manner. This is part of what it means to belong to a church.[13]

Belonging to a church makes possible gaining strength from the accumulation of its gifted witnesses, those who are known and those who are unknown.

Although these witnesses increase the credibility of what is handed on, they do not substitute for personal understanding. According to the maxim, faith seeks understanding. Those who have received what has been passed on do not only take it on the word of others who they recognize as living it "in a more complete, direct and powerful manner." They also desire to understand and integrate it for themselves.

We may not be in the same league as the saints, mystics, and unknown spiritually developed practitioners, but we want to play the game and move beyond spectator—out of the stands and onto the field. So we reflect on the prayer, working out the meanings of the symbols so we can say them with more dedication and authenticity. This never replaces the force that the language is given by those who lived it out in "complete" ways. But our efforts make the prayer ours, lesser light for sure but light nonetheless.

As we spelled out in "Translating Symbols into Meanings," these efforts of constructing and understanding appropriate meanings are necessary mental work. It confers an internal logic to the symbols that strengthens their reasonability. For example, one meaning associated with the symbol of "Father" is that the ones saying it are in union with an ultimate reality that is continuing to generate them at every moment. The result is a lessening of their fear in the face of suffering and death because their participation in life is eternally secured. This meaning is internally understandable: our God-groundedness mitigates the fear of loss. In fact, this meaning may be part of what we want to have in our minds and hearts when we pray the symbolic "Our Father." The consciousness it produces would definitely support the rest of the prayer. The inherited faith sought and found some understanding.

However, as inherited faith seeks understanding, understanding seeks realization. For example, Teresa of Ávila explains to her sisters the meaning of the soul in relationship to God: "there is 'someone' in the interior of the soul who sends forth these arrows and thus gives life to this life, and that there is a sun whence this great light proceeds, which is transmitted in the interior part of the soul. The soul . . . neither moves from that center nor loses its peace." This meaning of the soul may be able to be mentally grasped, but there is still another development. Teresa articulates it: "Oh, God help me! What a difference there is between hearing and believing these words and being led in this way to realizing how true they are!"[14] Meister Eckhart also speaks of this experience of knowing the understandings: "If a man dwells in a house that was beautifully adorned, another man who had never been inside it might well speak of it: but he who had been inside would *know*."[15] Understandings sow the seeds for realizations, the personal awareness that the words are not only logically coherent but describe a truthful spiritual condition.

While understandings have to be worked at, realizations often arrive—if they arrive at all—as a gift. The word "sudden" is often attached to them. Understandings are open to further reflection, dialogue, and even refutations. When something is realized, there is a self-evident quality to the moment of realization. It comes with its own credentials. Investigating it from another state of consciousness is possible, but this investigation seems most correct when it is drawing on its resources rather than questioning its actuality. In realizations, something is seen that may fade as consciousness changes, but part of the memory of its "moment" is its self-authenticating quality. That is why they are often evaluated as providing grounding, a place to stand and move out from and then return to. Realizations are subjective in the depth of their impact, but they also communicate a sense of objectivity, conferring solidness on the understandings that led to them.

The usual scenario is that realized understandings happen during prayer time and are often interpreted as moments of grace and/or inspirations of the Spirit. We are praying the Lord's Prayer and bringing into the symbols the meanings that are understandable to us and, suddenly, the truth of these meanings comes home to us in a powerful way. We are stopped and stunned and may find on our lips what Teresa found on hers: "God help me!"

However, my experience is that I have had realized understandings of the prayer meanings in non-prayer time. The prayer time prepared me, but life in the world made me realize the truth of the understandings. Then I brought those realizations back into the prayer time. In this way prayer and action became partners and revealed the full lineup: faith, understanding, realization, and—what we will consider now—integration.

Integrating into the Day

How long does it take to pray the Our Father?

Depends.

But no matter how short or long the time, the tension between prayer time and non-prayer time remains. Spiritual traditions are very aware of this tension. In particular, prophetic traditions point out the connections and disconnections between prayer and social action. The two are supposed to work together in ways that reflect the inseparability of the double commandment of love, love of God and love of neighbor. Prayer grounds the believers in the transcendent-immanent mystery of God and social action translates the ultimate intentions of this God into strategies of human dignity and common good. Prayer time and daytime are partners of private and public life.

Yet there is a tendency to think and act as if prayer is a self-contained activity, even if the structure of the prayer itself connects religious and social meaning. Prayer is an individual's raising of the mind and heart to God. There are many issues around this difficult activity and many ways to evaluate them. In fact, we can talk about our prayer life for a long time before we arrive, if we ever do, at how we act in our interpersonal, communal, and societal arrangements because of the way we pray.

Dietrich Bonhoeffer identified this tension between prayer and social action as "daily prayer" and the "day":

> Has it [daily prayer] transported her for a few short moments into a spiritual ecstasy that vanishes when everyday life returns, or has it lodged the Word of God so soberly and so deeply in her heart that it holds and strengthens her all day, impelling her to active love, to obedience, to good works? Only the day can decide.[16]

Far be it for me to bad-mouth a "few short moments . . . [of] spiritual ecstasy." In fact, I would stand in line with my hand out for any type of ecstasy. But prayer and action are meant to be held together. "Only the day can decide" is a good criterion for determining if, indeed, they are held together.

In one way, the Our Father is a prayer that is built for action. In the following three chapters we will describe it as having three sections. The first section ("Our Father who art in heaven") establishes the identity of the ones praying in the family images of beloved sons and daughters of our Father and brothers and sisters of all. The second section ("hallowed be thy name. / Thy kingdom come. / Thy will be done on earth, as it is in heaven") lays out the mission of these beloved sons and daughters of our Father and brothers and sisters of all to bring God's name, kingdom, and will into the affairs of earth. The third section ("Give us this day our daily bread, / and forgive us our trespasses, as we forgive those who trespass against us, / and lead us not into temptation, / but deliver us from evil") is the strategies of the mission. They include communicating love to vulnerable physical life, forgiving to find a new life beyond violence, and critically reflecting and praying the Lord's Prayer itself to resist temptation and evil. Therefore, praying the Our Father reinforces the identity, mission, and strategies of the beloved sons and daughters of the Father who are brothers and sisters of all. The prayer propels the ones praying into the world.

Yet, in another way, the prayer seems to be only distant background for social action. The identity needs to be clarified and internalized, the mission is vague and needs to be connected to specific situations and issues, and the strategies are more personalized orientation than the needed complex interpersonal and social analyses. In short, the prayer provides an ultimate stance that is on the lookout for proximate situations that might fall within its designs. According to my limited experience, this is a relatively correct appraisal of the relationship between prayer and action that is contained in the Our Father. It is also one of the reasons why these essential partners of prayer and social action often split apart. It involves quite a bridge to move from prayer time to the day that will decide.

But it is possible and it does happen. Prayer time internalizes the meanings of the phrases in an intentional way. This internalizing process creates structures of awareness in the mind. If the prayer has successfully embedded these structures, they enable the person to perceive situations and dynamics in those situations in a certain way. They facilitate discernments around "will," "kingdom," "bread," "forgiveness," "temptation," and "evil." Without those embedded structures of awareness, those situations and their dynamics may not come on the radar screen. Therefore, in prayer time we center, commit, and prepare.

Once this process has successfully gone on, actions in accord with the meanings of the prayer become possible. Once we act, we inevitably reflect on the action and its consequences. The reflection leads us back to the prayer and its meanings. Therefore, we are in a process of spiritual development. This moves from internalization to perception, from perception to action, and from action to reflection. Then the reflection returns us to the prayer where the meanings are developed and enhanced. In this way prayer and social action work together and strengthen one another. Therefore, the best way to appraise the Our Father is as prayer of preparation for action. In short, it is Jesus' prayer for discipleship.

Syncing Mind and Mouth

At the most basic level, praying the Our Father entails saying the words. This can be done either interiorly or out loud, either alone or with others. The assumption is what is in the mouth of the one praying is also in one's mind and what is in one's mind resonates with the mind of the prayer. Ken Wilber calls this the subjective fact:

> It is not what a person says, but the level from which they say it, that determines the truth of a spiritual statement. . . . [For example,] anybody can say, "All things are One," "All sentient beings possess Spirit," "All things are part of a great unified Web of Life." . . . *Anybody* can say those things. The question is, do you directly and actually realize that? Are you speaking with any sort of awakened authority, or are these just words to you?

When Wilber is asked, "What if they are just words? What does it matter?" he replies,

> Well, *spiritual realities* involve not merely statements about the objective world, but also statements of *subjective facts*, interior facts—and for those statements to be *true* when they come from your mouth, *you* must be directly in touch with those higher, interior facts, or else you are not being truthful, no matter how "correct" the words might sound. It is the subjective state of the speaker, and not the objective content of the words, that determines the truth of the utterance.[17]

Wilber's insight into subjective facts connects the mind to the mouth. When it comes to spiritual realities, the truth of the utterance is whether the one speaking is aware of those realities when the words that are meant to express and communicate them are coming forth from his or her mouth. Bringing forth revelatory words supposes awareness of the revelatory truths.

This is a high bar. It focuses on the realization moment in the continuum of faith-understanding-realization-integration. It entails considerable inner work to align the mind and the mouth. It demands a disciplined awareness both before and during speaking. This may be part of the Matthean Jesus' advice:

> When you pray, do not be like the hypocrites, who love to stand and pray in the synagogues and on street corners so that others may see them. Amen, I say to you, they have received their reward. But when you pray, go to your inner room, close the door, and pray to your Father in secret. And your father who sees in secret will repay you. (Matt 6:5-6)

First, he criticizes praying in synagogues and on street corners for all to see. This is using prayer, which should be a process of opening to God, as a blatant form of self-promotion. Second, he suggests going into your "inner room" to pray. This obviously undercuts seeking social approval for no one else is present. But it also facilitates the inner change of mind that is needed to correspond to the affective meanings of the prayer. The "inner room" is the deep self, the place from where the prayer should be spoken, the space where there is consciousness of the spiritual realities.

This criterion of "subjective fact" is particularly difficult when the spiritual statement is an inherited prayer. In chapter 1, we saw how the Our Father, because it is committed to memory at a young age, is prone to mechanical repetition. The words are mouthed, but no consistent attempt is made to tie the distracted mind to the meaning of the prayer as a whole or to each word and phrase in particular. If we take Wilber's advice and find ourselves praying the Lord's Prayer with this mindless inner state, we should stop. In the spiritual life, habit is a powerful force for both development and lack of development. When it decreases awareness during prayer time, it is a habit that should be broken.

Sometimes a way to modify the pull of mindlessness is to say the Our Father in another language. As a teenager, I learned it in the Greek of Matthew's gospel and in Latin. Down to this day, I will occasionally say the prayer or some of its phrases in those languages. Somehow this not-used-as-much language induces in me a more careful attention and takes my consciousness into considerations that deepen the praying experience.

Using alternate translations in English can also facilitate the syncing of mind and mouth. For example, Neil Douglas-Klotz's translation from the Aramaic of the Lord's Prayer moves the mind down new paths and forces thoughtfulness in speaking:

O Birther! Father-Mother of the Cosmos,
Focus your light within us—make it useful:
Create your reign of unity now—
Your one desire then acts with ours,
as in all light, so in all forms.
Grant what we need each day in bread and insight.
Loose the cords of mistakes binding us,
as we release the strands we hold
of others' guilt.
Don't let surface things delude us,
But free us from what holds us back.
From you is born all ruling will,
the power and the life to do,
the song that beautifies all,
from age to age it renews.
Truly—power to these statements—
may they be the ground from which all
my actions grow. Amen.[18]

This type of translation does not substitute for the standard version, but it provides insights that can be brought into the praying of the standard version. In doing so, it breaks the tendency of mindless repetition.

But, beside mindless repetition, there is another less than full engagement of the Our Father. When we pray the Our Father with devotion, our mind focuses on the transcendent source of all creation. God is being addressed and the mind struggles to adapt accordingly. However, the focus on God is vague and general. Often, the overriding attitude that permeates the prayer is worship. God is almighty, all-knowing, supreme, and so on. We are limited in every respect. Therefore, whenever we pray, we are always acknowledging a reality greater than ourselves. That is why we kneel and bow our heads during prayer. "Devotion" knows this truth and never lets it go.

If we find ourselves praying the Lord's Prayer with devotion, we should continue as long as we know there is a more developed way to proceed, and we walk that way from time to time. If we stay on the level of devotion, we will pray well in the community of believers. But there will be little or no transformation of consciousness, little or no spiritual development.

What Wilber is suggesting might be called "attention." Attention prays thoughtfully and concretely, savoring each phrase, allowing it to open the mind to God. It tries to adapt the consciousness of the one praying to the embedded consciousness of the prayer. Naturally, this means saying the prayer more slowly than is possible in community services. But it also means we will have to study the prayer as a prerequisite to praying it, developing meanings we discern as intrinsic to its authentic mind. If we spend time with the meaning of each phrase, then when we pray those phrases, the meanings will return accompanied by appropriate cognitive/affective states. Greater understanding of the meanings facilitates greater awareness in the act of praying, a more complete syncing of mind and mouth.

Conclusion

Praying the Our Father as a transformative spiritual practice is best situated within the Christian tradition of the imitation of Christ. It is assumed the prayer is a concise digest of the mind of Christ, a mind that can be appropriated by his followers who pray the prayer.

We prepare to make this mind of the prayer our mind when

- we recognize the mind of the prayer has the power to open us to Spirit;

- we develop the meanings of the prayer's succinct symbols in an accompanying language;
- we enter into the dynamic relationship of religious meanings motivating social actions;
- we use the language of petition to open ourselves to what is already being given and not to ask for divine intervention;
- we accept the interaction of faith, understanding, and realization as different but complementary moments of consciousness in our praying experience;
- we engage the movement toward action that integrates our prayer time with whatever the day brings;
- we bond our attention to the meanings of the words as we are actually praying them.

These seven challenges come with the territory of praying the Our Father. The language and structure of the prayer itself, the assumptions of its scriptural contexts, the history of its use among Christians, and our own personal and cultural ways of thinking and acting both precipitate these challenges and show us a way to deal with them. Once again, as with the seven challenges of transformative practices in general, they are not stumbling blocks. They are part of the path.

CHAPTER 4

The Identity of the Ones Praying

To pray "Our Father who art in heaven" with a consciousness that corresponds to the words is a bold and imaginative act. It entails prioritizing our spiritual identity within the complexity of the human makeup. We will explore this identity in five sections:

- Who Is Praying?
- Locating Heaven
- Finding Our Father
- Making This Identity Our Own
- We Dare To Say

Our spiritual identity is the foundation of the prayer, providing the motivation and energy for the mission and strategies that follow.

Who Is Praying?

In his book *What Is God?* Jacob Needleman tells the story of meeting the Zen master and teacher D. T. Suzuki in 1957.[1] Needleman was twenty-two years old, a philosophy major who had just written a paper on the self, blending many of Suzuki's ideas with the thoughts of Western thinkers. He was eager to impress and had formulated a question he wanted Suzuki to answer. He asked him, "What is the self?"

> I prepared myself to listen very carefully to his reply in order to carry the discussion further. Crowding the front of my brain, like devoted servants eagerly waiting to be called down to my lips, were Kierkegaard, Heidegger, Socrates, Immanuel Kant and many others.
>
> He smiled slightly with the left side of his mouth; and his bat-wing eyebrows twitched.
>
> "Who is asking the question?"
>
> I looked at him, dumbfounded. . . .
>
> "*I* am asking it!" I stammered like a fool, even with a shade of annoyance.
>
> "Show me this *I*," he said.
>
> Never had I felt more helpless. What the hell was he talking about? In fact, I actually felt a bit insulted.
>
> "What do you mean?"

Suzuki's return question, "Who is asking the question?" is the strategy of a Zen teacher, well-known now but not so well-known then.

However, it is also an answer to Needleman's first question, "What is the self?" Or, at least, it is a path to an answer. That Needleman is flummoxed, annoyed, and even angry is the mind's kneejerk defense system signaling this probe is not welcomed. Furthermore, when he insists "I am asking it" and Suzuki's return is "Show me this I," there is a sense of confusion and helplessness. If this is the path to enlightenment, it is not an easy walk.

But, in spiritual traditions, it is precisely this type of inquiry that turns consciousness inward or, perhaps better said, backs up consciousness into its "seat." The focus is not on what can be seen in the outer world, or bringing consciousness into the body, or holding it steady as it witnesses the ceaseless activity of the mind. It is coinciding with the one who is looking and saying rather than concentrating on what is seen and said. This concern with who is speaking and where the words are coming from is critical if praying the Lord's Prayer is to become a transformative spiritual practice.

Who is praying the Lord's Prayer? Where are these words coming from?

Discerning Symbols

The answer is in the first phrase of the prayer, "Our Father who art in heaven." But it is not a straightforward answer. This six-word opening takes the form of a direct address, ostensibly leading the mind to find and focus on the addressee and not the one who is saying the words. If we would take the phrase literally, we would be looking outside ourselves for an independent subject, albeit Divine, who has supplied our generative seed and who is located in the sky. Perhaps that is why a popular posture in praying this prayer is to lock hands with someone else (our) and look upward (Father in heaven). Although this literal approach appears to be faithful to the words, it may take our mind and imagination in the wrong direction. It overlooks the symbolic character of "Our Father who art in heaven."

The contemporary difficulties with these first-phrase symbols are well-known. The designation "our" looks to a larger group identity. Does it compromise the significance we give to the uniqueness of each person? Is the "I" lost in the emphasis on community and, even more, forgotten among a people who stretch far into the past? How can "our" signify the generating relationships that confer dignity on the uniqueness of each person who prays? Also, when we become specific, who does "our" include—our enemies, animals, our planet, the entire cosmos? How wide is "our"? Who do we think we belong to and what is everything of which God is Father?

"Father" is an image that is particularly suspect. It connects automatically to "child," or "son," or "daughter." Child may be immediately positioned on a continuum of child-adolescent-young adult-middle-aged, and so forth. It can connote dependence and immaturity, someone who is not ready for the important work of life. Therefore, "Father" is needed to provide guidance, a continuance from the biological fact that the father has already supplied seed. Does this symbol support a lack of full adult maturity, always looking for someone else to intervene and make the decisions about which we are unsure?

Also, "Father" is only one-half of the parenting duo. The absence of "mother" is striking and suspicious. As a God image, many have concluded that it supports male chauvinism and should be avoided among people who are striving for gender equality. Although the manifest objective of "Father" is to convey dependence, care, and even love, the latent functioning may be exclusivism. One strategy suggests the image be changed to "father-mother" or "parent." Other strategies suggest parental imagery is so ambiguous it should be avoided. "Father" is a symbol that permeates the gospels yet evokes many contemporary hesitations and challenges.

"Heaven" is equally ambiguous. It is an antiquated word for space. In contemporary minds it is not the highest sphere of a three-tiered universe that connects to earth by a periodic divine voice, or a descending cloud, or angelic visitations. And "earth" is not the flat land and sea under the sky. It is a planet in a galaxy among other galaxies. The first address of the prayer insists on the importance of the location of heaven; and the second set of phrases suggests that earth should emulate heaven. But, in the universe as we know it, is this a relevant way of talking, even with some sophisticated "hacking" of metaphors? If it is, what is it trying to convey?

With the Lord's Prayer, we have to negotiate the transmission of meaning from a past time with its inspired scriptural witness into a contemporary consciousness with different assumptions and ambitions. The original context of these images was a social ordering and a cosmology that does not reflect contemporary family and societal arrangements or scientific understandings of the universe. Also, over the centuries of its use in the Christian communities, the first phrase of the Our Father has accumulated a variety of associated meanings from different historical periods. Often these images and their inherited meanings linger on in the inherited consciousness even as they offend contemporary sensibilities. Some critics even evaluate them as having gone "rogue," contradicting the deepest intentions of the Gospel. The questions, "What do they mean?" and "How should we understand them?" naturally arise as a response to these qualms and critiques.

Therefore, as we proceed, we will have to carefully discern the meanings of the language of the whole prayer and, in particular, "Our Father who art in heaven." What are the meanings of these words we want to inform our minds, wills, feelings, and behaviors? This task is necessary, especially if we intuit this opening phrase is trying to communicate the deepest truth about us. In our time, the symbol of "Our Father who art in heaven" may have to give rise to a new set of thoughts and associations that disclose the deep identity of the ones praying.

Locating Heaven

The instructions of the opening phrase are clear but coded. "Our Father" is "in heaven." If we want to contact "Our Father," we will find that reality in heaven. This makes heaven a key symbol of the Lord's Prayer. It is the location of "Our Father" whose presence permeates and directs the entire prayer. Also, it is paired with earth, either immediately or eventually. This is not an accident, for heaven can only be understood when its interrelationship with earth (time and creation) is included. Also, heaven and earth mirror the dual makeup of the human person, paralleling the symbols of soul/body, spirit/flesh, and witty remark that humans are neither animals nor angels but a combination of both. So it is necessary to know where heaven is not only to find Our Father but also to find the fullness of ourselves and to grasp the mission of bringing heaven to earth. But, at this moment in the prayer, the emphasis is on heaven. This is where we will find the reality of "Our Father."

Heaven Within

When spiritual traditions focus on the human person, they usually point to a "deeper self," a "higher self," a "transcendent self," a "bottommost self," a "secret self," or a "real self." The introduction to *World Spirituality: An Encyclopedic History of the Religious Quest* describes this self as the *"inner dimension of the person called by certain traditions 'the spirit.' This spiritual core is the deepest center of the person.* It is here that the person is open to the transcendent dimension; it is here that the person experiences ultimate reality."[2] This is an important "locator" designation. Where the person "is open to the transcendent dimension" and "experiences ultimate reality" is within. Therefore, if "Our Father" is the Christian name for ultimate reality and ultimate reality is experienced within, then heaven, the location of "Our Father," is also within.

This certainly seems to be jumbled imagery that runs counter to the accepted meaning of heaven, which points "up" rather than "in." But spiritual teachers feel free to play with the symbols to loosen the mind and prepare it for new possibilities. Few play as freely as St. Isaac the Syrian:

> Enter eagerly into the treasure-house that lies within you, and so you will see the treasure-house of heaven; for the two are the same, and there is but one single entry to them both. The ladder that leads to the kingdom is hidden within you, and is found in your own soul. Dive into yourself and in your soul you will discover the rungs by which to ascend.[3]

According to these instructions, we have a "treasure-house within" that is the same as the "treasure-house in heaven." An "inner ladder to the kingdom" connects them; this ladder has "rungs" by which to ascend that you will discover once you are inside. All these images are meant to facilitate consciousness and participation in the immanent-transcendent Divine Mystery that is in and beyond everything. How do we do it? "Dive into yourself."

Walter Wink has similar advice and recommends we relocate "heaven" as a way to help our imaginations:

> Popular culture has tended to regard heaven (if it has regard for it at all) as a transcendent, other-worldly sphere qualitatively distinct from human life, to which the dead go if they have been good. What if we were instead to conceive of it as the realm of "withinness," the metaphorical "place" in which the spirituality of everything is "located," as it were. . . . Such a view of heaven finds it to be "nearer than breathing, closer than hand or foot," yet still transcendent.[4]

The poet Rainer Maria Rilke beautifully captures the benefit of this relocation. With height imagery, we could easily feel cut off from the great universe of which we are a part. He acknowledges this fear and quickly remedies it:

> Ah, not to be cut off,
> not through the slightest partition
> shut out from the law of the stars.
> The inner—what is it?
> if not intensified sky,
> hurled through with birds and deep
> with the winds of homecoming.[5]

When "intensified sky" is within, we are not lonely and separated beings playing earthly games in a stadium of unending space. We are not shut out from the law of the stars. There is not even a slightest partition between us. We are at home among them. Augustine connected this "in" and "high" in the most succinct way: *Deus intus, Deus altus* (God within, God above). When heaven is within, we are situating ourselves within both an immanent and transcendent Divine Reality.

Heaven Within as Deep Heart

Many traditions use the heart as a complementary symbol for heaven within. The physical heart is an organ that pumps blood throughout the body. The blood returns to the heart to be reoxygenated and then goes out to continue its life-giving work in the body. It is an activity of going forth, returning, and going forth again. This physiological functioning becomes a powerful image for our spiritual center.

Our spiritual center is the source and energy of life to that which it is connected—through the mind and body and into the world. But the energy is dependent on the center and has to return to it for revitalization. As a way of signaling that the physical pump is being used as an image for the spiritual center, the traditions say, "The heart is deep."[6]

Ken Wilber connects this deep heart activity with heaven and earth imagery and so brings it into the orbit of the Lord's Prayer. This imagery describes the heart's double relationship:

> In the traditions, Spirit is found neither in Heaven nor in Earth, but in the Heart. The Heart has always been seen as the integration or the union point of Heaven and Earth, the point that Earth grounded Heaven and Heaven exalted the Earth. Neither Heaven nor Earth alone could capture Spirit; only the balance of the two found in the Heart could lead to the secret door beyond death and mortality and pain.[7]

The spiritual center is the "union point" where the physical (earth) and spiritual (heaven) meet. It is not pure spiritual or pure physical but their interconnectedness. They are mutually beneficial to each other. Heaven finds the grounding it needs and Earth finds the exaltation it desires. The deep heart is the place of connection. When it functions this way, it becomes the "gate of heaven and earth."

Evelyn Underhill elaborates this imagery of "heaven and earth" in philosophical concepts:

> We are, then, faced by two concepts, both needful if we are to make any sense of our crude experience; the historical, natural and contingent; the timeless, supernatural and absolute. They must be welded together, if we are to provide a frame for all the possibilities of human life; and that life, whether social or individual, must have both its historically flowing and its changelessly absolute sides. . . . Doubtless, the mass of men, such consciousness is still in the rudimentary and sporadic stage. Here and there it does appear among us, though in very unequal degrees. And in so far as we are aware of these two aspects in ourselves

and in the universe, we have to strike a working balance
between them, if we would rightly harmonise the elements
of life and achieve a stable relation with reality.[8]

These two dimensions—heaven and earth—are both in us and
in the universe. They are characterized as the timeless and the
historical, the supernatural and the natural, the absolute and
the contingent. This is the "given" of the human condition.

However, awareness of this "given" is not uniform. It appears in unequal degrees. In most it may be "rudimentary
and sporadic." Yet full human potential is dependent on this
awareness, for these two dimensions need to be worked with
to develop a "weld[ing] together," a "working balance," and a
harmonizing of the elements. The result would be "a stable
relation with reality." This is what the Lord's Prayer suggests
when it proposes heaven is brought to earth. Heaven and earth
are not just side-by-side realities. They are partners in an integration process.

Heaven Within as Soul with Two Eyes

But how does this harmonizing, welding, balancing of
heaven and earth take place? To take a step in this direction,
some have brought forward and developed the idea of soul.
But, in the history of spirituality there is an immediate danger
associated with this idea. It has often brought the mind into
heaven and left it there. Earth is what needs to be fled to arrive
at and stay in heaven rather than what needs to be transformed
by the presence of heaven. The transcendent dimension of the
human is valued and cultivated, but it becomes an end in itself.
So caution must be exercised.

Even though soul is understood as the spiritual center
"within," it should not lead to a neglect of "without." As the
late-eighteenth-century German poet Novalis wrote, "The
seat of the soul is where the inner world and the outer world

meet. Where they overlap, it is in every point of the overlap." In fact, the one "who can see the inward in the outward" is more spiritual than the one "who can only see the inward in the inward."[9] The soul is the pivot between the spiritual (God) and physical (mind, body, world), between the inner and the outer. Since the soul's relationship to its spiritual Source is so critical, it must be emphasized; but this focus should never obscure its "pivot position."

This "pivot position" is captured in the imagery of two eyes. The soul has the capacity of looking in one direction and then in another. "The . . . created soul of man has two eyes. One represents the power to peer into the eternal. The other gazes into time and the created world."[10] The overlap is not so complete that both "heaven and earth" merge into each other, but they are intimately intertwined.

Spiritual traditions hold the eye that peers into the eternal has priority. "The essence of the soul, for Christianity, and that which constitutes its worth, is its being the organ of communion with God."[11] This sense of worth is strengthened by the perception that the relationship to the eternal lasts and the relationship to the temporal fades. "Do not store up for yourselves treasures on earth, where moth and decay destroy, and thieves break in and steal" (Matt 6:19). Therefore, common sense, energized by the often denied but persistent drive for immortality, stresses the soul looking into eternity. Although this drive is often interpreted as the frightened ambition of the ego, much more than that is going on when we suspect life does not end with the death of the mind-body.

However, another reason for the priority of the soul looking into the eternal, and the one that we want to stress, is that the Spirit it receives from the eternal is what it brings into the world of historical activity. The nature of the spiritual is its ability to enter into what it is not and elevate what it enters into all it can be. Spirit is the ultimate source of full human potential. When it does that, we recognize the excellence in what the Spirit inhabits and name those abilities "gifts of the Spirit" or "fruits of the Spirit." The two dimensions of "heaven and earth" are held together by the spiritual because the agenda of the spiritual is to weld, harmonize, and create balance, to bring into excellence everything it informs. The book of Wisdom describes this activity: "[B]ecause of her pureness she pervades and penetrates all things. . . . Although she is but one, she can do all things, / and while remaining in herself, she renews all things" (Wis 7:24, 27, NRSV).

Finding Our Father

Therefore, the deep heart that holds together heaven and earth and the soul with two eyes are symbols of the makeup of the human person. Our natural inclination is to put together these symbols in this way: we are finite beings (the earth side of the deep heart and the eye of the soul that peers into time and creation) who are in an intimate relationship with the infinite (the heaven side of the deep heart and the eye of the soul that peers into the eternal). We are most familiar with earth/time-creation side (our psychological, physical, social, and cosmic dimensions), and so it is the normal and comfortable place to begin. We are least familiar with the heaven/eternal side, and so it is second to be considered. After we have exhausted the resources and adventures of the earth/time-creation, we reach into the little known heaven/eternal. Most of us go to "our Father in heaven" with tentative steps.

But the dare of the Lord's Prayer, part of its transformative invitation, is to reverse this normal way of proceeding. It asks us to start with the heaven side of the deep heart and the eternal eye of the soul. If we can do that, the prayer will facilitate bringing together the dimensions of the whole person to cooperate and act as a unity. When we coincide with the heaven side of the deep heart and the eternal eye of the soul, we receive Spirit from the infinite. The nature of this Spirit is to suffuse and perfect the finite, the earth side of the deep heart and the time-creation eye of the soul. "Spirit makes all things one." In the language of the prayer, the heaven side is where we find Our Father; and that is the wild and ultimately unimaginable reality that lures us into further transformations. Nikolai Grundtvig captured this positioning of where the words of the prayer are coming from in a short poem: "Only God's true children have a mouth / To call God their Father / From the ground of the heart."[12]

Crying Out "Abba!" in the Spirit

What exactly happens on the heaven side of the deep heart and in the eye that peers into the eternal? According to St. Luke and St. Paul's understanding of "Father," there is an intimate and profound intermingling of the Divine Spirit and human spirits.

In Luke's gospel when the disciples ask Jesus to teach them to pray, he begins with a word of direct address, "Father" (Luke 11:2). Commentators point out this simple, straightforward opening connotes a sense of intimacy and nearness. There is neither formality nor the attribution of many titles. The mouth opens and from the inner depths "Father" emerges. This is a word of abundance from the heart (Luke 6:45). Jesus is not calling out to someone who is absent. The reality of "Father" is close at hand. It is more a matter of attention, of opening consciousness to the divine presence. Therefore, this simple beginning critiques all prayers weighted with protocol and presupposing a distant, aloof, difficult-to-contact deity.

Paul delves deeper into this sense of intimate divine presence, and the mediation and companionship of Jesus, in the act of praying. In Romans 8:16-17 he writes that when "we cry, '*Abba*, Father!' [t]he Spirit itself bears witness with our spirit that we are children of God, and if children, then heirs, heirs of God and joint heirs with Christ, if only we suffer with him so that we may also be glorified with him." In Galatians 4:6-7, similar dynamics are emphasized: "God has sent the Spirit of his Son into our hearts, crying, 'Abba! Father!' So you are no longer a slave but a child, and if a child then also an heir, through God." Although Paul does not spell out a complete prayer, the exclamation "Abba! Father!" goes to the heart of the full text in Matthew.

Once the transcendent-immanent Mystery is imaged as "Abba! Father!" the whole range of family imagery comes into play. Since we can say "Abba! Father!" we are obviously children of God. Since the Spirit we have received is the Spirit of the Son, we are brothers and sisters to Jesus (the Son). Also, as children we are not slaves but heirs. In fact, we are heirs of God and joint heirs with Christ and we share in his life and destiny—"we suffer with him so that we may also be glorified with him." This collection of images—Abba! Father!, Son, children, heirs—work together to express and communicate the Christian revelation.

Importantly, the crying out of "Abba! Father!" is not an arbitrary designation. Its experiential genesis is the awareness of Spirit to spirits communication. "God" can be interpreted as a name for the vast, unknowable Mystery that is the origin and destiny of all things. (We will explore this more in the phrase, "hallowed be thy name.") But when the Spirit arrives from this Mystery and suffuses our spirits, we recognize its creating reality. The nature of the Mystery has been revealed as a giver of Spirit and, as such, a generator of the spirits of those who receive it. We cry out, acknowledging God in the intimate image of "Abba! Father!" For Paul, this is obviously an ecstatic utterance, driven by the awareness that the Divine Spirit is awakening our spirits and bringing us to life.

Therefore, "Abba! Father!" is the expression of a consciousness of spiritual generation. However, I doubt this is the usual prayer experience for most people. Appointed prayer times with calm recitals of prescribed words may miss this passion, this drive to express an exploding interior awareness. There may be times when praying the Our Father is accompanied by inspiration dynamics that are the same or similar to Paul's Spirit-induced phrase of "crying out." But most of the time they are not. The day-in, day-out practice of praying the Our Father is more a matter of persevering in a commitment than bursting with a revelation.

However, even when we are not aware of Spirit-generation, Spirit-generation is present and at work. The "aware times" are special and can be remembered and reentered at other times. They become resources for the more ordinary times of prayer. But they also reveal a metaphysical structure, an enduring condition. Ecstatic utterances do not have to be the constant consciousness of our prayer life, but it should be assumed they reveal an abiding truth. The Spirit of God is continually creating the human spirit in each individual. This makes our spiritual being essentially relational. If we center ourselves in this truth, we can authentically cry out "Abba! Father!" at any time.

> At this stage of our reflection, who is praying the prayer?
>
> When we open our awareness to the heaven side of the deep heart and the eye that peers into the eternal, we are receivers of the Divine Spirit that empowers our spirits to cry out "Abba! Father!" This conviction pushes us to say we are children of God and brothers and sisters of the Son (Jesus) and we share his mission and destiny. This is who we are when we say, "Our Father who art in heaven."

But, as important and revealing as this is, more has to be said. This further development is implied in Paul's description, but it is so critically important it needs to be lifted out and highlighted. These Spirit-suffused children of God who are praying can also be further designated as "beloved sons and daughters of our Father."

Beloved Sons and Daughters of Our Father

Whenever I attend baptisms, usually infant baptisms, I always have the sense more is going on than I am able to take in. I follow the words and symbols and participate when the ritual says I should. But something inside me is always whispering, "Stop and ponder." Although the rite reflects a long history of baptismal debates and is a mixed bag of theological agendas, it is saying something very significant about the child and the commitments of parents, godparents, and the church. For me, the message is always connected to and mediated through baptism of Jesus. In fact, as Christians, everything we are and can become is through our participation in the event of Jesus Christ. Therefore, we do baptisms because what happens to Jesus in the baptism narratives of the Synoptic Gospels is meant to have parallels in our lives.

Each account of Jesus' baptism is different and the differences reflect important perspectives (Matt 3:16-17; Mark 1:9-11; Luke 3:21-22). But the basic message is this: the heavens open and a voice says Jesus is God's beloved son and his pleasure runs through him ("in whom I am well-pleased"). This baptism is the inaugural event that propels Jesus into his mission. If I let my imagination loose, I see this infant who is surrounded by the gathered community of believers in the same position as Jesus—poised to hear the voice of love that will propel him or her into the mission of his or her life. Of course, the child cannot have a conscious experience of this voice of love. Rather it lies in the future and is part of the promise of the parents, godparents, and the church to instruct the child in practicing the faith.

Beatrice Bruteau suggests one of these training practices. As Christians who always seek to grow in faith, we might meditate on Jesus' baptism and experience the heavens opening and the voice speaking to us:

> Listen to the Voice. Don't think about it, just listen to it. Feel good, listening to it. "Beloved," it says. "Delighted with you," it says. Hear that, stay with that, sigh and relax with that. Don't let yourself introduce reasons why it shouldn't be so. The Voice doesn't make conditions or exceptions. It's an absolute assertion of loving you . . . Repeat this meditation every chance you get. Remember it in between times. Live with it. Live from it.[13]

This meditation exercise tries to bring home to us the truth of our own baptism. If we can hear and internalize this heavenly voice, we may begin a path of understanding, realizing, and integrating our beloved status. All who are present at baptisms are encouraged to pray the Lord's Prayer at the conclusion. Hearing the voice of love has empowered them to say the words of love.

Therefore, this voice from heaven is dramatically powerful and it targets what is most important in the fullness of our human makeup. However, as provocative as it is, more needs to be said. The fuller reach of the voice from the opened heavens is developed in the voice of another God image, the father in the parable of the prodigal son. This well-known story is summarized as follows:

- The younger son asks and gets his inheritance from his father.
- He immediately goes into "riotous living" in a far country and discovers the nature of money: it runs out.

- Reduced to taking a job feeding pigs, he would eat with the pigs, but no one offered. The bottom.

- At the bottom comes the brainstorm. "In my father's house even the servants have enough to eat. I will go to my father and say, 'Father, I have sinned against heaven and you. Do not take me back as a Son, but as a hired hand.'"

- Demotion script in place, he makes for the house of his father.

- While still a long way off, his father sees him, has compassion on him, and begins to run. He embraces him and kisses him.

- The son begins to recite his rehearsed script with his reduced status. But the father will not let him finish. Instead, the father says to the servants, "Quick! Bring the best robe and put it on him; put a ring on his hand and shoes on his feet. Kill the fatted calf, and let us eat and make merry. My son was dead and has come back to life; he was lost and now he is found."

There is more to the story, the significant more of the older brother, but the father who talks from the sky and says, "Beloved son and daughter" has spoken again. In his words to his prodigal son, belovedness is given a depth and permanency that boggles our mind and makes us realize we are dealing with something completely other from the ordinary ways of the earth.

We are not strangers to the prodigal son's hangdog script. It is one thing to screw up; and it is another thing to think we are the screwup. The real problem is not the riotous living or the company of pigs. It is thinking that these disasters have replaced the "son at the center." But it is a mistake we have a tendency to make. We embrace what we have done wrong as our defining moment. Other people are only too willing to help us do this to ourselves, never letting us get too far away from our egregious errors. We ink a pact of punishment in the secret center of ourselves. We turn ourselves into hired hands.

The Father will have none of it. His first word is "Quick!" Something must be done before the prodigal's temptation to identify with his negative behaviors and his wrongheaded mental conclusions are solidified. Perhaps the robe, ring, shoes, feast, and messages of eternal rebound—the lost are found and the dead come back to life—will do it. In other words, the father always sees and calls to his son and daughter. The point is clear: the father never stops loving the son and daughter even when the son and daughter misidentify who they are and stop loving themselves. In shorthand, the father is compassionate and merciful.

This belovedness-no-matter-what is our baptismal identity, and it is the foundation for how we pray. Before we say, "Our Father who art in heaven," the Father in heaven has said "beloved son and daughter." The heavens speak to us before we speak to the heavens. Also, the father never stops seeing and calling to this beloved son and daughter no matter what we have done or how we and others evaluate who we are and what we deserve. We are someone we cannot not be—the beloved son and daughter. This is because the immanent-transcendent Mystery of Love will not let us ultimately identify with any other dimension of ourselves, in particular the actions and conditions of sin that do not reflect our beloved status. We may give up on ourselves, but "in whatever our hearts condemn us, . . . God is greater than our hearts" (1 John 3:20).

Therefore, when we pray "Our Father who art in heaven," the "in heaven" location signifies both our inner openness to transcendence and the strangeness and everlastingness of the life and love we receive from that Source. In the ways of the earth, relationships are contingent upon proper behavior. They can be broken and lost, a set of dynamics the older son in the parable strongly defends (Luke 15:25-31). But the Father's love plays by a different set of rules. It is a fierce fidelity to the essential truth of who we are in relationship to God.

> At this stage of our reflection, who is praying this prayer?
>
> When we open our awareness to the heaven side of the deep heart and the eye that peers into the eternal, we are receivers of the Divine Spirit that empowers our spirits to cry out "Abba! Father!" We are also ones who hear the transcendent voice of love and know we are beloved sons and daughters of our Father. Although we are prone to think we can lose this belovedness, the One who creates the love and life never abandons us. This is who we are when we say, "Our Father who art in heaven."

This takes us further along the path of identifying who is praying the Our Father. Our spiritual identity is essentially relational. Our spirits are continually receiving life and love from the Spirit of our Father in heaven. As unimaginable as this may seem to ordinary consciousness, there is a next step that furthers the prayer's transformation agenda for the mind. The dare has more in store.

Brothers and Sisters of All

A transliteration of the opening words of the Greek of the Lord's Prayer (Matt 6:9) is "Father of us." This phrasing has the advantage of placing "our" after "Father." As we have elaborated, to say "Father" is empowered by our awareness that we are receivers of life and love from the Spirit of the Divine

Source. However, even though we may be praying the Lord's Prayer alone, we do not pray "my Father." The realization that arises simultaneously with our communion with God is our interdependency with everyone and everything that is also in a substantial relationship with God. The reality that sustains and suffuses us sustains and suffuses all people, living and dead. Even more, this Divine Reality sustains and suffuses all creation. Therefore, we are brothers and sisters of all, and we verbalize this truth by praying, "Our."

The paradoxical path to "our" is through coinciding with the spiritual depth of ourselves. When we do this, we surprisingly see ourselves as plural, more than a limited and separated self. As the truth of our dependence on the self-giving love of the Father deepens, the hold of separateness that our physical, psychological, and social dimensions have bequeathed to us loosens. In our core we are a double-relationality.

First, we are in communion with and in dependence on the immanent-transcendent Mystery of life and love. Second, from that perspective, the world in which we live begins to look different.

> God cannot be found or grasped in the external world, but only in the inner world. If we seek him outside, we shall find him nowhere; if we seek him within, we shall find him everywhere. This is not to say that only the inner world is real. Both are real; both have their own measure of importance. But it is the inner world which has the priority and the greater importance. . . . Having discovered God within, we can then discover him without; but never the other way round.[14]

Discovering God within translates into discovering God without. More specifically, realizing our identity is an act of receiving life and love from the immanent-transcendent Source gives us the "eyes" to see all of created reality as receiving their being from the same Source. In the encyclical *Laudato Sì*, Pope Francis calls this the "sublime communion."[15]

This connection to all creation might be hidden in the literal Greek of Paul's crying out, "Abba! Father!" In the Greek text there is a definite article before "Father." A literal translation would read, "Abba! The Father!" Abba denotes the Source that is the personal grounding of the ones praying. "The Father" would mean the same Source sustains all people and creation. Therefore, we become brothers and sisters to all creation since all creation is flowing from and dependent upon the same Source that is our ultimate identity.

This sense of interdependent communion among all people broke through to Thomas Merton in his famous vision at the corner of Fourth and Walnut: "I was suddenly overwhelmed with the realization that I loved all these people, that they were mine and I theirs, that we could not be alien to one another even though we were total strangers. . . . There are no strangers!"[16] Later, he will articulate this sense of communion with all as "being one with everything in the hidden ground of Love for which there can be no explanations."[17] In other words, it is simply a given that can be seen when the mind is properly disposed. It is not something that, in the first moment, is argued to through a series of explanations. Primarily, it is a manifestation. Secondarily, the logic of the manifestation can be laid out.

In his *Asian Journal*, Merton talks directly to all and calls us "my dear brothers and sisters, . . . we are already one. But we imagine that we are not. And what we have to recover is our original unity. What we have to be is what we are."[18] This is a cousin to Albert Einstein's famous quote:

> A human being is part of the whole, called by us "Universe;"
> a part limited in time and space. He experiences himself,

> his thoughts and feelings as something separated from the
> rest—a kind of optical delusion of his consciousness. The
> striving to free oneself from this delusion is the one issue
> of true religion. Not to nourish the delusion but to try to
> overcome it is the way to reach the attainable measure of
> peace of mind.[19]

This is quite a claim. Unity among people and the planet is
not an ideal to be pursued. To mystical consciousness, it is a
present reality. The problem seems to be we are not aware that
unity is the ground of our separate condition.

But besides our underlying unity with God and creation,
there is also another present reality. Merton was acutely aware
of this reality and dedicated to changing it. This is the reality of violent and destructive actions between people and by
people toward the planet. Both these realities are included
in the Lord's Prayer and are part of what is symbolized by
"heaven and earth."

An old Hasidic story tries to bring home the intercommunion of all people:

A rabbi asks his students when they could tell night had
ended and day had begun. This is an important moment, for
the beginning of day is a time for prayer.

"Is it when you can see an animal in the distance and tell
whether it is a sheep or a dog?" asked one student.

"No," the rabbi answered.

"Is it when you can see the lines on the palm of your hand?"
asked another student.

"No," the rabbi answered.

"Is it when you can look at a tree in the distance and tell
whether it is a fig or pear tree?" asked a third student.

"No," answered the rabbi.

"Then how can you tell when night is over?" the frustrated students asked.

"When you can look on the face of any man or woman and see that they are your sister or brother, then morning has broken. Until then, it is night."

In some ways "brothers and sisters of all" is a commonplace thought and accepted with a conventional shrug. But when it is a morning revelation that breaks the darkness with light, it shocks our complacencies and repositions us in a radical way.

> At this stage of our reflection, who is praying this prayer?
>
> When we open our awareness to the heaven side of the deep heart and the eye that peers into the eternal, we are receivers of the Divine Spirit that empowers our spirits to cry out "Abba! Father!" We are also ones who hear the transcendent voice of love and know we are beloved sons and daughters of our Father. Through this communion of life and love with the Father, we are also brothers and sisters of all, interdependent with other people, living and dead, and all creation. This is who we are when we say, "Our Father who art in heaven."

Really?

Making This Identity Our Own

With the help of Scripture and tradition, we have a picture of who is praying the Lord's Prayer. However, it is one thing to pull images and ideas from the rich resources of Scripture and tradition, especially the mystical tradition, and quite another thing to make them our own. This spiritual identity may seem fantastical. It is certainly not the usual way we identify ourselves.

If we are asked who we are, most likely we bring forward one or more of the available selves that we embrace in our daily life. We identify with our gender, or our sexual orientation, or our age, or a physical or mental suffering or characteristic, or a social role or work position, or membership in a race, a nationality, or a family, or with some trait or collection of traits of our personality. We are quick and comfortable with naming characteristics of our physical, psychological, or social being as identity markers. And that would be correct and appropriate—as far as it goes. But none of these identities are completely in sync with saying, "Our Father who art in heaven," and the dynamic structure of the entire prayer. The identity the prayer proposes through its imagery is often not on our radar screens.

However, it is on the radar screen of some people. There are those who see our transcendent selfhood with remarkable clarity. Ken Wilber relates a shopping mall experience:

> Yesterday I sat in a shopping mall for hours watching people pass by, and they were all as precious as green emeralds. The occasional joy in their voices, but more often the pain in their faces, the sadness in their eyes, the burdensome slowness of their paces—I registered none of that. I saw only the glory of green emeralds, and radiant buddhas walking everywhere, and there was no I to see any of this, but the emeralds were there just the same. The dirt on the sidewalk, the rocks in the street, the cries of the children, here and there—a paradise in a shopping mall, and who would ever have suspected?[20]

"Who would ever have suspected?" asks Wilber, acknowledging our penchant for lesser identities. In all honesty, I usually need someone to help me suspect. What Ken Wilber's consciousness did not register, I would have picked up on and, most likely, would have been stuck on.

But Thomas Merton would have suspected. More, he would be nodding his head in agreement. His mystical experience on the corner of Fourth and Walnut was not only about the intercommunion of people, as we described above. It also included a vision of the deep spiritual center of every human. He suddenly sees "the secret beauty of their [people's] hearts, the depths of their hearts where neither sin nor desire nor self-knowledge can reach, the core of their reality, the person that each one is in God's eyes."[21]

But he is not sanguine about people knowing this about themselves. "If only they could all see themselves as they really *are*. If only we could see each other that way all the time." His hesitancy reflects Evelyn Underhill's evaluation that this double structure of reality is in most people only rudimentary and sporadic. Merton is suggesting it should become sophisticated and continual. If it were known, "there would be no more war, no more hatred, no more cruelty, no more greed."[22] In other words, we would bring this heavenly identity onto the struggling earth to heal and transform it. Quite frankly, I find this prediction too facile. But I certainly think this is the consciousness to which we have to hold fast and pursue its implications.

Although we may be neither Wilber nor Merton, we want to heed their vision because it seems so in tune with the mind of the prayer. But we must appropriate it in terms of our own lights and not fall into any type of mimicry. This process of making it our own picks up many of the lessons of transformative spiritual practices—working with resistance, being patient with gradualness, revisiting fundamental desire, and persevering in the practice. It also incorporates one of the most

important Christian challenges of praying the Our Father—
using the continuum of faith, understanding, realization, and
integration.

This identity begins and is sustained by faith. It is the gift
of others, inherited from the Christian tradition. The fact of
this inheritance is a permanent aspect of making it our own.
However, as understanding deepens, the sense of this identity
"being mine" increases. With more understanding, the mysti-
fying gives way to genuine Mystery. Then breakthroughs may
arrive—either in prayer time or outside prayer time—that confer realization. We see it directly, and know Teresa's difference
and have seen the inside of Eckhart's house or at least peeked
through the window (see chap. 3). New behaviors open up for
us, behaviors we never saw before; or, if we did see them, we
only saw them in retrospect, after the opportunity had passed.
But no matter to what degree this happens or does not happen,
the faith basis permeates the whole process. If we live patiently
and humbly on the continuum, we may find this consciousness
of the heaven side of deep heart and the eye of the soul that
peers into the eternal becomes increasingly available.

I think persevering in the prayer brings about more confidence that we are spiritual beings and greater practicality in
how to open our minds to Spirit and cooperate with its energies. Meditating in and through the Lord's Prayer transfers its
consciousness into us. Consistent practice gradually grounds
what at first might seem an unexperienced vision of who we
are. Although the prayer is always challenging, we move into
risking more and more involvement with this interpretation
of who we are. The mind of the prayer validates itself the more
we trust it and move at our life situations out of its energies.

However, the prayer is always happening within a life of
many happenings. Some of these other happenings work in
tandem with the prayer to confirm its assumptions and chal-

lenges. Three of these happenings that I have found helpful in awakening to our spiritual identity are engaging in other forms of meditation, encountering spiritually developed people, and reflecting on our experiences of courage and love.

Meditation

Although spiritual practices in general and meditation exercises in particular vary widely and have different goals, most of the ones I have tried contribute in one way or another to shifting consciousness to a deeper spiritual identity and experimenting with how to see and act from that identity.[23] Beatrice Bruteau, who insisted on a personal realization of our spiritual identity, suggests a meditation exercise that brings the users into their spiritual center. Bruteau calls this center, "I AM/MAY YOU BE":

> Think of answering the question, Who are you? Make a list of answers: I am gender, race, nationality, religion, work, marital/parental status, and all the rest of the description. Now try to sit firmly in the I AM part of the sentence, to feel yourself *be-ing* in those ways. Next, alter the description; if you are tall, imagine yourself short; if contemplative, active; if irritable, patient; and so on. Then, take away the descriptive items, one by one, while remaining clearly and vividly aware of *be-ing*. Try to work down to just a few very general descriptions; then begin to erase them, acting from the central position of I AM. . . . You may be able to let them all loose, remaining in the I AM without any following predicate, without any modification.
>
> If you can do this [dis-identify with the descriptive selves], you will discover something amazing: just as in a solar eclipse, the solar disc disappears little by little and everything gets darker and darker, until at the moment of totality the solar corona breaks forth in all its glory—just

> in that way, when you work your way down to the bare
> undescribed I AM, . . . your radiance will suddenly erupt,
> and you will find that the I AM is also MAY YOU BE! This
> central, undefined *be-ing* is you, the *person*.[24]

If we try Bruteau's instructions, they might help us understand and realize our deeper identity of communion with God
and creation and the dynamics of those relationships. With
meditation exercises the proof is in the pudding. This is not
standard spiritual advice, but when we know the goal, it is legitimate to experiment with ways to get there. The goal is to
bring us into awareness and conformity with the identity that
articulates itself as "Our Father who art in heaven."

Spiritually Developed People

Besides meditation practices, we can remember people
who called out in us the "beloved son and daughter of our
Father who is in heaven." These are usually spiritually developed people who have this effect in a simple and disarming
way. They become our spiritual teachers because when they
talk to us, they talk to our spiritual identity. They see the territory of our physical, psychological, and social trademarks,
but they speak from the spiritual center of themselves and to
the spiritual center in us. In chapter 2, we identified spiritual
teachers as both a specific class of people and any people who
through what they say or how they live awaken and inspire
us to open to the spiritual dimension. I suspect every life has
spiritual teachers. Sometimes they are credentialed professionals. But most often they are significant people in our lives
who, besides being a parent or relative or friend or neighbor,
bless us by reminding us who we are.

The question is, are we alert to them? Do we hear their words
and see their actions and take them into ourselves or do we
shrug them off? Some spiritual traditions assert there is a world-

wide conspiracy to wake us up to our spiritual identity. If that is the case, there are incognito spiritual teachers everywhere.

Eknath Easwaran credits his grandmother with awakening him to the spiritual life. He describes her as a woman who was free and taught him the path of freedom.[25] Once, when he was a schoolboy, the teacher in his local school pushed home a scientific fact that in those bygone years in India was little known or accepted. The earth was round. It was a truth that disturbed Easwaran. But when he told his grandmother, "not a hair fell out of place." She simply said, "What does it matter? . . . You can be selfless whether the earth is round or square or triangular."[26] She reminds him of his deeper spiritual identity that is the source of selfless action. Whatever the facts are about the earth, the spiritual truth of himself is what always has to be remembered and lived.

Rachel Naomi Remen's grandfather matches Easwaran's grandmother. As a little girl, he always called her "Neshume-le," which means "beloved little soul." With him Rachel felt a powerful acceptance. "I was already enough. And somehow when I was with him, I knew with absolute certainty that this was so."[27] The depth of this acceptance is revealed in an incident when they disagreed. It revolved around what constitutes a minyan.[28] A minyan is a group of ten men who, when they are gathered together, constitute an official prayer service. These ten men were the holy ground of Judaism. Rachel asked why it could not be ten women, and her grandfather insisted the law said ten men. But when her grandfather was sick and dying, she would often hold his hand. Once when he woke from sleep and saw her, he said, "You are a minyan all by yourself, Neshume-le." Her grandfather told her the truth about herself.

But even with spiritually developed people always appearing with reminders of our spiritual identity, we need discipline and attention to reflect on those significant moments. Often those moments begin a process more than they establish a permanent breakthrough in consciousness. Words are said or actions are taken, and we see clearly what had formerly been obscure or not known with such precision. But this moment of awakening can disappear as quickly as it comes. We do not seem to produce them as much as they arrive unbidden. That is one reason we often refer to them as "grace."

Therefore, the transiency of these experiences means they are never completely captured as they are happening. They need to be hosted in memory and pondered. What we dimly realized at the moment has to find words, even if the words are stumbling and in need of further refinement. We must eat the truth of the spiritual identity that came our way and internalize its wisdom.

For example, Piero Ferrucci was a student of one of the founders of psychosynthesis, Roberto Assagioli. One day he told Assagioli that he thought following our feelings was the attitude toward living we should all assume. Assagioli looked at him and said, "But you must *not* follow your feelings. Your feelings must follow *you*." This remark stunned Ferrucci. But what is crucial is not only the remark itself but the mental activity that followed it:

> I was taken aback by this remark. After all, I thought, weren't we all supposed to be listening more to our feelings, which were so often brutally repressed or maltreated in our over-achieving society, thus accounting for so much of the psychological malaise we see around us? Surely we had to give in fully to the natural demands of our emotional life. That was my credo. And here was this old man telling me that my feelings had to follow *me*! How authoritarian, how unfamiliar that sounded! At the same time, the statement—perhaps because of the disarming way it had been uttered—awoke my curiosity. I soon realized the importance of the problem. Should we acknowledge

our feelings as the primary factor in deciding what to do
in our various life situations? And if not, which part of us
should determine our course of action?[29]

It is not the teaching itself. It is the wrestling with the teaching, allowing it to interact with existing mental conditioning,
following the questions it raises into modified ways of thinking, willing, feeling, and acting. Waking up to our spiritual
identity is a process of attending and reflecting. When we
do that, we facilitate our ability to situate our consciousness
in the spiritual truth about ourselves; and, in doing that, our
spiritual teachers and their teachings contribute to our ability
to pray the Lord's Prayer.

Experiences of Courage and Love

Besides meditation and spiritual teachers, another way
we suspect a spiritual identity is at work is by noticing and
reflecting on some of the ways we act. Our behaviors are not
always rational acts, thought out beforehand and executed by
design. Nor are they only habituated behaviors, doing what we
are accustomed to doing. Sometimes we find ourselves acting
in a certain way and wonder where the action comes from,
the whence of our behavior. When we trace the inspiration
and energy of these actions to their source, it can be a path of
awakening to our spiritual identity.

Paul Tillich pointed out one of these types of actions in
philosophic language and described the dynamics he thought
energized it. He called it the "courage to be." Finite human beings are continually threatened by nonbeing. Yet they affirm
the meaning and worth of their finite being in the face of the
forces of nonbeing that surround and permeate them. This
self-affirmation is possible because they are spiritually participating in the ground of being.

> To Tillich . . . the life, vitality, and creativity in us [come
> from] an infinite source; they rush and push *through* us,
> and they culminate in our creative and expressive being,
> our behavior, our powers, our acts, and our ability to be.
> The creature *is* in and through the infinite power, order,
> and meaning of being that rush through her or him, and
> the possibilities that lure and impel him or her into active
> being. In all of our aspects we *are* through our intimate
> relation to the infinite power of being and meaning which
> is being-itself, or God.[30]

Therefore, when finite being demonstrates its capacity to affirm life in spite of all its negativities, it is due to the spiritual
source "rushing" through us.

My guess is most of us know this experience of courage.
But we probably have not given it Tillich's profound interpretation. We have all dealt with threats to our finite being. Our
health might be precarious, our mental condition anxious
and fearful, our interpersonal relationship deteriorating, our
economic status shaky, our work demeaning, and so on. We
know the forces of nonbeing.

We also know we can find responses that are more than
capitulation to these negative forces. We may find them in
cooperation with others and with the unforeseen arrival of for-
tunate circumstances. But these creative responses also have
a dimension of interiority. They always entail drawing upon
some inner resource. We are more than our physical, psychological, and social dynamisms and their positive and negative
features. As the fourteenth-century Persian poet Hafez said,
"I wish I could show you when you are lonely or in darkness
the astonishing light of your own being."

Besides the experience of the courage to be, we often back
into our spiritual identity through the unfolding dynamics of
love. A standard distinction of theological literature is between

erotic love and agapic love. Erotic love is attracted to another, but this attraction is basically a way of seeking its own good. Agapic love is attracted to another but seeks the good of that other. The two often come together in the course of a love relationship.

We often begin the love adventure by being attracted to the physical, psychological, and social features of the beloved. We seek to be united to those features because of the "good" that is in it for ourselves. Eros is in the ascendency. But over time our knowledge of the other increases and the desire to be with them and for them deepens. We become committed to the beloved and their well-being in a way that puts into second place our own egocentric desires. Yet strangely this lack of self-focus does not translate into us lacking anything. We find that giving ourselves to another in companionship and support does not diminish us. In fact, the more we give ourselves to another to increase their being, the more our own sense of being increases. We become who we are by giving ourselves to another. Agape is in the ascendency.

The emergence of agape is a tipoff our spiritual identity has been engaged. Since our spiritual identity is receiving life and love from the Divine Source at all times, it is secure and full. It naturally overflows into the world with the same type of love and life that it is receiving. As we notice this is going on, we sense we are more than a bundle of needs looking for fulfillment. Our deeper spiritual self is manifesting itself and in the manifestation—just like when green grows in the desert in the Sufi story of chapter 2—there are instructions about how to cooperate and continue the manifestation.

It is not only the Lord's Prayer that solicits our spiritual identity and wants it to be the content of consciousness. Indications that we are beloved sons and daughters of our Father are present in our meditation practices, our interaction with people who are spiritually developed, and our experiences of courage and love. When all these come together, something about them, even when we do not know the whole of them, resonates so deeply we know we cannot escape. They beat on the drum of our heart from the inside; and since we ultimately know this music is partly of God and partly of our own making, we cannot refuse the dance. We venture to become who we most deeply are.

We Dare To Say

The identity of the ones praying is expressed when they authentically pray, "Our Father who art in heaven." This address is surely what the traditional invitation says it is—a dare to say. So it is often kept in the background, brought out only when there is sustained insistence we justify why we are doing what we are doing and why we will not be persuaded to do otherwise. However, in a contemporary culture of full disclosure and transparency, we should not be overly hesitant. It is a matter of integrity, and finding our voice around this level of articulation is one of the effects of our prayer practice. Going public with who we are (and, in fact, who everyone is) is a sensitive self-disclosure. It takes time to be both comfortable and effective in communicating it. If it is a "wild" appreciation for us, it may register "crazy" for others.

But this identity makes praying the Our Father less pedestrian. As a dare, it intimates an adventure is in the offing. This is not something ordinary, predictable, or normal. We are going to say something we should overhear ourselves saying because it is proposing a challenging agenda. W. H. Auden caught the flavor of this dare in his Christmas oratorio, *For the Time Being*:

He is the Way.
Follow him through the Land of Unlikeness;
You will see rare beasts, and have unique adventures.[31]

"Rare beasts" and "unique adventures" is a promise that is maddeningly imprecise and may strike us as either inviting or intimidating. But, whatever else it is, it is not business as usual.

However, the Lord's Prayer is not a dare to the "ego," asking us to do great things and receive plaudits from the troops. Slaying dragons is out. It is not a call to conventional consciousness to do more of what it already knows and entertain the heroic as much as it can. Rather the prayer is a steady and unrelenting invitation for consciousness to go deeper, to coincide with the heaven side of the deep heart and the eye of the soul that peers into the eternal. In this "space" the Divine Spirit and our spirits fuse, and in this spiritual communion we cry out "Abba! Father!" We know ourselves as beloved sons and daughters of our heavenly Father and brothers and sisters of all.

Although this identity may not be our normal comfort zone, the prayer asks us to stretch into this self-understanding. This stretch is necessary; and although complete alignment may be gradual and hesitant, the desire to pursue this fullness cannot be halfhearted and on-again, off-again. If we do not suspect and come to understand "Our Father who art in heaven" implies the deepest truth about us, we will have nothing to bring to earth. The rest of the prayer will not be the freedom of the beloved sons and daughters of our heavenly Father to act in new ways. It will be a recital of hapless and confusing directions we do not understand and cannot follow.

However, as we coincide more and more with our spiritual identity, we fulfill what Paul considered a longing of creation. "For creation awaits with eager expectation the revelation of the children of God" (Rom 8:19). But even the revelation of the children of God has a further element of mystery in it. Saint John remarks, "Beloved, we are God's children now; what we shall be has not yet been revealed" (1 John 3:2). Although we know the present reality of our identity as beloved sons and daughters of our Father who are brothers and sisters of all, we do not know where this is taking us. The mission and strategies of the prayer give us a glimpse.

CHAPTER 5

The Mission of
the Ones Praying

Our ultimate, spiritual identity is located on the heaven side of the deep heart and the eye of the soul that peers into eternity where, empowered by Spirit-generation, we cry out "Abba! Father!" and know ourselves as beloved sons and daughters of our Father and brothers and sisters of all. The packed, opening words, "Our Father who art in heaven," symbolically capture this identity. They generate a relational consciousness that situates us as receiving life and love from the Divine Source and through that Source living in communion with all other humans and the rest of creation who are also receiving life and love from the Divine Source.

However, no sooner are those opening words spoken than a process of going out from that identity unfolds. We move from the heaven side to the earth side of the deep heart and from the eye that peers into eternity to the eye that peers into time and creation. We will explore this movement and the changes in consciousness it entails in these sections:

- From Heaven to Earth
- Hallowed Be Thy Name on Earth
- Thy Kingdom Come on Earth
- Thy Will Be Done on Earth
- Deepening the Dare

Therefore, when we say these words of mission, we carry heaven into the affairs of earth and commit ourselves to a trio of struggles that deepens the dare.

From Heaven To Earth

In the Our Father, the dynamics of inner spiritual identity and outer social mission are fused together and symbolized as "on earth, as it is in heaven." It is assumed that the person praying has access to both heaven and earth and has the capability of moving from one to the other. This is a swing of consciousness and it is embedded in the act of praying where we can "dwell" in heaven and envision what bringing heaven to earth might entail. The assumption is that "name, kingdom, and will" are grasped and appreciated in their heavenly modality. This is the eternal state of affairs; and we can intuit enough of it to know it is the vision we want to espouse for the earth where these realities are not in the developed state they are in heaven.

In the chapter on "The Identity of the Ones Praying," we located heaven within. Therefore, the movement from heaven to earth can also be imaged as a movement from the inside to the outside. In "As kingfishers catch fire," Gerard Manley Hopkins articulates this movement from identity to mission in a provocative and insightful way:

As kingfishers catch fire, dragonflies draw flame;
    As tumbled over rim in roundy wells
    Stones ring; like each tucked string tells, each hung bell's
Bow swung finds tongue to fling out broad its name;
Each mortal thing does one thing and the same:
    Deals out that being indoors each one dwells;
    Selves—goes its self; *myself* it speaks and spells,
Crying *What I do is me: for that I came.*
I say more: the just man justices;
    Keeps grace: that keeps all his goings graces;
Acts in God's eye what in God's eye he is—
    Christ. For Christ plays in ten thousand places,
Lovely in limbs, and lovely in eyes not his
    To the Father through the features of men's faces.[1]

This is a hymn to our spiritual identity-mission dynamics, the inside-out process. All mortal things are driven by the same energies—to fling out broad their names. They are dealing out the being that "indoors dwells" because selves, by their nature, "goes its self." As they speak and spell themselves, they cry out the essential truth they cannot contradict: "What I do is me: for that I came." Those who cry out "Abba! Father!" know the propulsion of this unstoppable exclamation.

However, the hymn does not stay on this natural level, so to speak. It is driven to say more. The more is the overflow between the spiritual center of the person ("just man," "Keeps grace," "what in God's eye he is") and its manifestations ("justices," "keeps all his graces going," "Acts in God's eye"). This process reveals the person as Christ, playing in ten thousand places and generating loveliness in the physical features of people, manifesting the spiritual center in the psychological, physical, and social selves. This play is energized by interior grace and is a movement to the Father. "Our Father" is not only the source of these initiatives but also their destination.

However, the poem does not focus on the struggles involved in moving from heaven to earth, from transcendent identity to mission, from the inside to the outside. Heaven as heaven is not fully present on earth. Therefore, it has to be brought into the scattered mental states, the vulnerable physical conditions, the conflicted social situations, and the unpredictable cosmic environments of the earth.

This does not mean heaven replaces earth and obliterates the finite conditions of historical existence. This is not an end-time new heaven and new earth scenario. Also, it does not mean heaven is brought into the earth without any change in consciousness or language. Although heaven is a consciousness that can be inhabited on its own terms, the journey into earth demands it be translated into earthly forms. To be relevant to the earth, the consciousness of heaven has to speak the language of the earth. Therefore, heaven and earth are distinctive yet intertwined dimensions of awareness that live and flourish in dialogue with one another.

A good example of this process of heaven-earth interaction is a Buddhist meditation text from the Sutta Nipata:

> May all beings be filled with joy and peace.
> May all beings everywhere,
> The strong and the weak,
> The great and the small,
> The mean and the powerful,
> The short and the long,
> The subtle and the gross:
>
> May all beings everywhere,
> Seen and unseen,
> Dwelling far off or nearby,
> Being or waiting to become:
> May all be filled with lasting joy.

Let no one deceive another,
Let no one anywhere despise another,
Let no one out of anger or resentment
Wish suffering on anyone at all.

Just as a mother with her own life
Protects her child, her only child, from harm,
So within yourself let grow
A boundless love for all creatures.

Let your love flow outward through the universe,
To its height, its depth, its broad extent,
A limitless love, without hatred or enmity.

Then, as you stand or walk,
Sit or lie down,
As long as you are awake,
Strive for this with a one-pointed mind;
Your life will bring heaven to earth.[2]

It is not until the last line of the meditation that we are told the desires and directives of the text reflect the process of bringing heaven to earth. But, once that imagery is used, we can reread the meditation from that perspective.

First, it says "out loud" what the one meditating is about. It immediately launches into its agenda for the earth. Motivation and commitment are out in the open. They are not unknown nor are they hidden beneath specific actions. The depth of the acting person is disclosed. The heavenly self is in touch with the underlying equality of people and so desires the joy and peace of all beings, reflecting this consciousness of universal communion. This universality is extensively, even wittingly, laid out. The strong, great, powerful, long, and subtle are not given preference. They are paired with their opposites—the weak, small, mean, short, and gross. The evaluative ways of the earth that separate opposites and compare them are not employed. All are wished peace and joy.

Also, deceiving and despising others coupled with the anger and resentment that wishes and enacts suffering is refused. No matter how commonplace these ways are and how conditioned we are to engage in them, they are not to be followed. The one meditating has learned something in heaven that makes these strategies unacceptable. The ones who say these meditative words strengthen their commitment to bringing equality and nonviolence to the earth.

Second, if this way of heaven is to be successful, it must be internalized and developed. We have to let our love grow until it has a mother's passion, becoming boundless and flowing out into the close and far reaches of the universe. This entails eliminating enmity and hatred in ourselves. This expansive language reveals the love we are cultivating is not the creation of a finite being. This love is the infinite Mystery manifesting itself through our finite being. Only God can be the source of a love with this outreach in time and space. The ones saying the words are in service of something greater that is flowing through them.

Third, it is intimated that staying awake to this universal love consciousness is a difficult task—"as long as you are awake." But if we can, everything we do, even physical motions—sit, lie down, stand, walk—will feel and conform to the heavenly influence. Moving from heaven to earth is more than a matter of determining issues our heavenly identity should select and address, although that is necessary. It is a matter of personal transformation—the physical, psychological, and social being suffused with Spirit.

This text is meditated on in the morning. Who knows what the day will bring? But grounded in this consciousness, we are ready, not to be seduced into what is happening on the surface but to discern the opportunities for dignity and reconciliation and engage those opportunities with skill and creativity. In this imaginative language, heaven comes to earth mediated through person and situation.

Therefore, this meditation text with its heaven to earth structure prepares us for praying the mission of the Our Father with its heaven to earth structure. Praying the mission will entail a clear and strong statement about our motivations and commitments and how they meet the needful conditions of the earth. This will include grounding these motivations and commitments in the depth and outreach of divine love and realizing the difficulty and importance of staying awake to this level of consciousness with its drive to personal transformation as well as overcoming social divisions and enmities. In moving from heaven to earth, we are embedded in a process we have the capacity not only to cooperate with but to direct.

Hallowed Be Thy Name on Earth

The Forgetting Earth

Spiritual traditions often paint the earth/world in distinctive yet denigrating colors. These portraits do not show everything, but they point out the limitations and failures of the dominant ways of thinking and acting. These weaknesses provide the openings for what the beloved sons and daughters want to bring to earth. Heaven meets earth in precisely those places where earth is distorted.

A story called "What Is the World Like?" characterizes a particular limitation of the earth and a condition with which the beloved sons and daughters have to deal:

> God and a man are walking down the road. The man asks God, "What is the world like?"

God replies, "I cannot talk when I am thirsty. If you could get me a drink of cool water, we could discuss what the world is like. There is a village nearby. Go and get me a drink."

The man goes into the village and knocks at the door of the first house. A comely young woman opens the door. His jaw drops, but he manages to say, "I need a glass of cool water."

"Of course," she says, smiling, "but it is midday. Would you care to stay for some food?"

"I *am* hungry." he says, looking over his shoulder. "And your offer of food is a great kindness."

He goes in and the door closes behind him.

Thirty years goes by. The man who wanted to know what the world was like and the woman who offered him food have married and raised five children. He is a respected merchant and she is an honored woman of the community. One day a terrible storm comes in off the ocean and threatens their life. The merchant cries out, "Help me, God."

A voice from the midst of the storm says, "Where is my cup of cold water?"

The answer to the title of the story "What Is the World Like?" is this: The world is a place of forgetfulness. It is God who is forgotten. "Our Father who art in heaven" is not given any real attention. We do not have time to give God even a mere cup of cold water. This is a story line most of us know only too well.

We are legitimately busy with many things. The physical and social conditions of our lives demand all our attention. They tire us out, bring us to sleep, and then return the next day to rule our time and our minds. In Luke's story of the Great Feast, people do not accept the invitation to the feast because they have to tend to their land, their animals, and their families (Luke 14:15-24). Their excuses are memorable:

"I have purchased a field and must go to examine it."

"I have purchased five yoke of oxen and am on my way to evaluate them."

"I have just married a woman, and therefore I cannot come."

Needless to say, the man of another parable who was busy building barns to hold more harvest also could not make the feast (Luke 12:16-21).

There is a wonderful Hindu depiction of this preoccupation with the material and social demands of life. Rachel Remen uses it to great effect in her book *Kitchen Table Wisdom*.[3] Joseph Campbell, the noted mythologist, is conducting a workshop for doctors, showing and commenting on sacred images from world religions. One of them shows the god Shiva dancing in a ring of bronze flames. His many arms hold symbols of abundant spiritual life. One foot is up in the air and one foot is positioned on the back of a little man who is bent over, totally absorbed in studying a leaf. The doctors were taken with the little man and asked Campbell about him. Laughing, Campbell told them the little man was so engrossed in the material world that he did not even know the living God was dancing on his back. In our culture, to varying degrees, we are all that little man.

The point is not to disparage these wonderfully drawn characters or ridicule their normal set of worldly concerns. It is their total preoccupation that the parables and the Hindu image target. The point is, with our heads down we will not respond to the invitation of heaven's feast. We will miss out on what we are meant to participate in. Metaphorically speaking, we will not give God a cup of cold water. Therefore, God cannot tell us what the world is like. Of course, in one way God does not have to tell us. We have already experienced its power to absorb and limit consciousness by monopolizing our attention with the immediate demands of the earth.

Forgetfulness of God is not the memory loss of one particular entity, even if it is characterized as a Supreme Being.
Forgetfulness of God is simultaneously forgetfulness of our
true self, the exclusion of who we really are. The Epistle of
James makes this connection. Its major concern is stated: Why
is it people only hear the Word but do not do it? If we are only
hearers, we are like "a man who looks at his own face in a mirror . . . sees himself, then goes off and promptly forgets what
he looked like" (Jas 1:23). Forgetting this, they cannot live in
the "perfect law of liberty." This is the capacity to bring the
freedom of love to situation after situation. Instead, they are
condemned to conform to the external fate these situations are
imposing. The bottom line to the earth's forgetting of God is
enslavement to whatever is happening. The ones praying the
prayer propose another way—a remembering consciousness.

Hallowing

In the face of this tendency of the earth to forget God, we
pray to hallow the name of "Our Father who art in heaven."
However, hallowing is not a mental and affective consciousness that is as natural as forgetfulness. But it is something
those who have been to heaven see as a necessary truth to
remember and live out in time and creation. When heaven
comes to earth and brings the benefits of heaven with it, it
translates into the activity of hallowing.

To hallow something is to do more than honor it, or respect
it, or recognize its significance. To hallow something is to
make it, in the phrase of Paul Tillich's, our ultimate concern.
As our ultimate concern, it energizes our actions. No matter
what we think or do, it is always somewhere in the mix. It
is embedded in our makeup and essential to our being; it is
something we cannot "be" without. If we question what we
think and do long enough and hard enough, it is the final "why"
we arrive at. In short, it is the activity of holding something

sacred and not allowing it to be sidelined by either the best or worst of what befalls us.

This psychological-spiritual act of hallowing is connected to "thy name." According to the prayer, the name we are hallowing is "Our Father who art in heaven." But we immediately have to acknowledge "Our Father" is in "heaven." In this context, the image of heaven indicates the essential mysteriousness of this identity. "For as the heavens are higher than the earth, / so are my ways higher than your ways, / my thoughts higher than your thoughts" (Isa 55:9). We cannot expect to capture this reality with mental constructs and prosecute it according to what is logical and reasonable to us. It does not fit into our knapsack. We may be Spirit-generated children of God and beloved sons and daughters of the Father, but we always remain creatures who never fully plumb the Mystery of Love, the intercommunion of all beings with Holy Being and with one another.

Thy Name

The phrase "thy name" carries this connotation of essential Mystery. When "name" is applied to God, it suggests we are dealing with more than we can know and our proper response is trust rather than a demand for complete comprehension. When there is a revelation of the name of God in the Scriptures, there are usually some circumstances to suggest the revelation is not complete. Although the revelation is true as far as it goes, there is still more to the reality of God than is revealed. Revelation is always in tandem with concealment.

For example, in the famous scene of Moses and the burning bush that does not burn out, God tells Moses that he is the God of the Israelites' ancestors and their deliverer from misery and injustice (Exod 3). This is a revelation, but Moses still pushes the question of his name. When God replies, "I am who I am," or in another translation, "I will be with you as who I am will I be with you," commentators continually point out this is an answer that is not an answer.[4] Rabbi Lawrence Kushner paraphrases what God said to Moses is what God always says: "I'm sorry but I can't help you; I'll be whatever I'll be. Alive and real. And therefore unpredictable."[5] Actually, God does provide a revelation but avoids giving the impression Divine Reality is an object of human knowledge and can be dealt with as other objects of human knowledge. Although the revelation is true, there is more reality than the revelation makes known.

Later in the exodus story, a similar lesson unfolds. Moses asks to see God's glory. God lays out the conditions: "But you cannot see my face, for no one can see me and live. . . . When my glory passes I will set you in the cleft of the rock and will cover you with my hand until I have passed by. Then I will take away my hand and you shall see my back but not my face" (Exod 34:20, 22). When God's glory passes before him with its announcement of forgiveness and mercy, we know we have not left the realm of mystery but entered it more deeply. As important as this revelation is to the future of the covenant, it still suffers from incompleteness. Seeing the "back of God" is a wonderful image that a full, "face-to-face" encounter is not available.

Therefore, "name" signifies there is more to God than any specific naming can capture and communicate, a condition mystics continually stress.[6] But there is more to the idea of Mystery than just greater concealment. Mystery is also related to the revelation itself. What was made known in itself is a mystery, pushing our cognitive and affective capacities to their limits and leaving us with a sense of not being able to go further.

How is God present as who God is? How is God a liberator of those who suffer injustice? How can the bush burn without burning out? How can God completely inhabit creatures without displacing them? How is God merciful and forgiving without eliminating the dynamics of the just consequences of actions? How is God loving each individual and bringing all together in a communion of love that includes all creation?

If hallowing means we must remember God on an earth that tends to forget God, then hallowing "thy name" means we must remember "Our Father who art in heaven" as an essential Mystery of Love, an intercommunion that makes beloved sons and daughters and brothers and sisters to all. Abraham Joshua Heschel knew the position this puts us in:

> For just as man is endowed with the ability to know certain aspects of reality, he is endowed with the ability to know that there is more than what he knows. His mind is concerned with the ineffable as well as with the expressible . . . What the sense of the ineffable perceives is something *objective* which cannot be conceived by the mind nor captured by imagination or feeling, something real which, by its very essence, is beyond the reach of thought and feeling. What we are primarily aware of is not our self, our inner mood, but a transubjective situation, in regard to which our ability fails. Subjective is the *manner*, not the *matter* of our perception. What we perceive is objective in the sense of being independent of and corresponding to our perception. Our radical amazement responds to the mystery, but does not produce it. You and I have not invented the grandeur of the sky nor endowed man with the mystery of birth and death. We do not create the ineffable, we encounter it.[7]

There is something ineffable about the full reality of the human condition. This is not a weakness or an evolutionary moment that further development will eliminate. When we allow it in, it can have the effect not of diminishing us, but of enriching and emboldening us. Christian Wiman, in reflecting on his cancer sufferings, discovered this difference:

What is the difference between a mystery in which, and by means of which, one's whole spiritual and intellectual being is elated and completed, and a mystery that merely deflates one's spirit and circumvents one's intellect? . . . What I crave—and what I have known, in fugitive instants—is mystery that utterly obliterates reality by utterly inhabiting it, some ultimate insight that is still sight. Heaven is precision.[8]

On the earth "Our Father who art in heaven" is a Mystery of Love that "elate[s] and complete[s]" our "spiritual and intellectual being." This gives it a strange type of "precision" because it responds directly to what we "crave." However, in all honesty, for most of us we probably do not know this is what we need until those "fugitive instants" arrive and teach us both the need and the fulfillment at the same time.

Hallowing the name of "our Father in heaven" invites us to center ourselves in this reality and trust its darkness as an even greater love than what has come to light. Even though we do not have full knowledge of its ways, when we open to its reality, it makes us fully alive. As we walk the earth with its tendency to forget God, we pray "hallowed be thy name" and we remember the Mystery of Love that holds us individually and collectively. Praying the prayer establishes and cultivates this remembering consciousness.

Thy Kingdom Come on Earth

The Dominating Earth

Spiritual traditions have more to say about the earth than it is a place of forgetfulness. In fact, it is more commonly characterized as a situation where sin is rampant, where the commitment and embodiment of Our Father's name, kingdom, and will are mightily resisted and almost never found. This is so deep and pervasive a human condition that the Christian tradition has called it "original." When earth is seen from the viewpoint of heaven, more than anything else it is a condition that seeks a redemption it cannot manage by itself.

The Christian imagination of R. S. Thomas captured this desperate situation of earth and heaven's desire to help in his poem "The Coming." God and the son are having a conversation in heaven:

> And God held in his hand
> A small globe. Look, he said.
> The son looked. Far off,
> As through water, he saw
> A scorched land of fierce
> Colour. The light burned
> There; crusted buildings
> Cast their shadows; a bright
> Serpent, a river
> Uncoiled itself, radiant
> With slime.
> On a bare
> Hill a bare tree saddened
> The sky. Many people
> Held out their thin arms
> To it, as though waiting
> For a vanished April
> To return to its crossed
> Boughs. The son watched
> Them. Let me go there, he said.[9]

Heaven and earth are connected, two sides of the deep heart. When we view earth from the vantage point of heaven, we immediately become aware of how earth is hurting and how we are called to change it. We feel the compassionate pull of "Let me go there." The relational consciousness of heaven, our true identity, is contradicted by the separatist and antagonistic situations of the earth. We are establishing and cultivating a change consciousness.

This sinful situation of earth is classically described as estrangement. It is what happens when we turn away from God and one another and turn in on ourselves. This turning in on ourselves and making ourselves the measure of everything is hubris. Hubris results in concupiscence, pulling everything into ourselves to gain importance and safety. Therefore, sin is the scenario of the separate self, estranged from God and others and doing everything it can to assuage this anxious condition of vulnerability.

This underlying sinful condition generates multiple negative personality traits and behaviors. The Christian tradition has never hesitated to list them. Paul enumerates, "They are filled with every form of wickedness, evil, greed, and malice; full of envy, murder, rivalry, treachery, and spite. They are gossips and scandalmongers and they hate God. They are insolent, haughty, boastful, ingenious in their wickedness, rebellious toward their parents. They are senseless, faithless, heartless, ruthless" (Rom 1:29-31). The seven deadly sins—pride, avarice, envy, wrath, sloth, gluttony, and lust—continue this tradition. Of course, the imaginative horrors of hell are the full blossoming of sin.

However, a more targeted take on sin identifies two overlapping effects. Sin grants dignity only to those who have certain gifts and possessions and structures society so that these few possess and control the majority of material and social goods. This renders most people undignified and permanently bereft of essential resources. Also, since these gifts and possessions are seen as scarce, they are highly valued and pursued aggressively. Violence becomes the natural way of the earth. Those who dominate have dignity and possess as much as they can. Those who are dominated have no dignity and possess only enough to survive in order to serve and produce more for those who dominate.

This situation is the polar opposite of the relational consciousness of "Our Father who art in heaven." In the consciousness of heaven the Father is loving each person into existence in every moment, and that is the source of his or her dignity. So dignity is essential and equal in all people. Also, each person is related to every other person. In fact, through their common dependence on Divine Reality they are indwelling in one another, receiving and giving life and love to one another. The implication of this heavenly, metaphysical truth is that essential dignity of all and mutual universal care should be the social condition of the earth. The material and social goods of the earth should be distributed justly.

Therefore, when heaven with its agenda enters the sin of the earth, it moves with the two principles that Catholic social teaching has stressed—human dignity and common good. But these principles are not welcomed in the way the earth is constructed. In fact, they are a threat to be disregarded; and if they are pursued too aggressively, they are attacked with the goal of eliminating them. As the gospels spell out in detail, there are ramifications for those who bring the kingdom of God with its vision of human dignity and common good into the kingdoms of the earth that are committed to another rendition of how the world should work.

Thy Kingdom

In *The Last Week*, John Dominic Crossan and Marcus Borg contrast two processions on Palm Sunday. Coming into Jerusalem from the west were Pontius Pilate and the soldiers, representing the kingdom of Rome:

> Imagine the imperial procession's arrival in the city. A visual panoply of imperial power: cavalry on horses, foot

soldiers, leather armor, helmets, weapons, banners, golden eagles mounted on poles, sun glinting on metal and gold. Sounds: the marching of feet, the creaking of leather, the clinking of bridles, the beating of drums. The swirling of dust. The eyes of silent onlookers, some curious, some awed, some resentful.[10]

Coming into Jerusalem from the east was a "prearranged 'counter-procession'" of Jesus, representing the kingdom of God (Luke 19):

> So they brought [the colt] to Jesus, threw their cloaks over the colt, and helped Jesus to mount. As he rode along, the people were spreading their cloaks on the road; and now as he was approaching the slope of the Mount of Olives, the whole multitude of his disciples began to praise God aloud with joy for all the mighty deeds they had seen. They proclaimed:
>
>> "Blessed is the *king* who comes in the name of the Lord.
>>   Peace in heaven and glory in the highest." (vv. 35-38)

The contrast is blatant, imaged as the horse compared to the colt (Zech 9–10), war compared to peace, the king in Rome compared to the king who comes in the name of heaven. With the contrast comes the potential conflict, a conflict the Jewish elite does not want:

> Some of the Pharisees in the crowd said to him, "Teacher, rebuke your disciples." [Jesus] said in reply, "I tell you, if they keep silent, the stones will cry out!" (Luke 19:39)

But the conflict cannot be avoided. It is grounded beyond the silence and shouting of people. It is built into the very stones.

When the kingdom of God comes from heaven to earth, it arrives on an earth that already has multiple kingdoms. The political, social, and economic structures of these kingdoms are built on the powers of division and accusation and the people within them have internalized the thoughts, feelings, and behaviors to legitimate these structures and make them work.[11] This combination of social structures and formed people are usually not open to alternatives, especially the people on top who are doing very well by the way the present social structures are set up. In the story of Jesus the structures and formed people of Rome, Judea, and the temple priesthood combine to do away with Jesus' challenge, leaving the lasting impression in Christian life that living and advocating for the kingdom of God leads to a deadly push-back. To live the kingdom is to suffer the cross of the empire.

The cross, of course, was a punishment inflicted by the imperium on those who threatened its existence. It was imposed as the price of noncompliance with the prevailing kingdom of Rome, and it was the earthly fate of Jesus. However, the startling response of the followers of Jesus, based on Jesus' own response, was not to keep silent and be safe. The natural response of avoidance was not sanctioned and advocated. Instead, the proactive advice of engagement was brought forward.

The followers of Jesus were to integrate suffering and rejection into the dynamics of living and advocating for the kingdom of God. "[Jesus] said to all, 'If anyone wishes to come after me, he must *deny himself* and *take up his cross daily* and follow me'" (Luke 9:23, emphasis added; see also Matt 10:38; Mark 8:34; Luke 14:27). There is a lot compressed into this rendition of the conditions and consequences of following Jesus and his mission of bringing the kingdom of God.

First, it involves denying and refusing to comply with some form of ourselves ("deny himself"). What is the self that has to be avoided? To live the kingdom of God is to be committed to the second half of the following pairs: first/last, exalted/humbled, dominate/serve, revenge/forgive, punishment/mercy, exclusion/inclusion, ignore/help, violence/peace. Many of the stories, sayings, and injunctions of the gospels portray these alternatives and make strong cases for the second half of the pairs.

However, the first half is deeply ingrained. Those attitudes are embedded in people the kingdoms of the earth have formed; and nobody is completely free of their influence. Therefore, the self that must be denied is the one who seeks to be first, exalted, and violent and prefers to dominate, retaliate, punish, exclude, and ignore those who would jeopardize their agendas and plans.

In the gospels, the difficulty of choosing the second half is highlighted by the fact that this first half is found in the disciples. It is not just Jewish and Roman leaders and those who have no use for this type of disjunctive question and the choice it imposes. It is all who are in the kingdoms of the earth and have internalized these attitudes, including the disciples who are struggling to move from the first half to the second half. The kingdoms of the earth have formed them. Therefore, following Jesus often results in how Mark describes the disciples: "They were on the road, going up to Jerusalem, and Jesus was walking ahead of them; they were amazed, and those who followed were afraid" (Mark 10:32, NRSV).

This situation of the disciples in the gospels is the perennial situation of disciples. We who dare to follow Jesus always have to deny ourselves. When we pray "Thy kingdom come," the way we think about ourselves and our ingrained habits of thought and action immediately come under scrutiny. The kingdoms of the earth have formed us and so there is always a tension between the first and second halves of those behavioral pairs. Of course, we would like to ignore the whole issue. We would rather criticize the outlandish actions of others and analyze social structures for their deep biases.

But "Thy kingdom" commitment suggests personal transformation is always a component. In fact, it is the sustaining energy of social change. "Why do you notice the splinter in your brother's [or sister's] eye, but do not perceive the wooden beam in your own eye?" (Matt 7:3). The reason is, we can see the splinter in our brother or sister's eye better than we can see the beam in our own eye. Self-knowledge is always more difficult than criticizing others.

Besides personal transformation according to kingdom values, Jesus demands his followers engage in an ongoing way the individual and social conditions that persecute kingdom of God living ("take up his cross daily"). On one level, what this means is, do not be deterred when people do not understand and refuse to make the changes the kingdom of God suggests. Remember the relentless widow who eventually forced the unjust judge to come across with justice. Why? "She is wearing me out."[12] Taking up the cross includes suffering, but it is not courting suffering. It is forging ahead against individual and social resistance.

On another level, it means not being coopted by the violent ways of the kingdoms of the earth. There is always a tendency to fight fire with fire. But "Thy kingdom" will never come by outdoing the kingdoms of the earth on their own terms. But the temptation to do this is so strong it becomes a designated strategy of the Lord's Prayer—"lead us not into temptation." We will explore this strategy in the next chapter.

When we pray "Thy kingdom come," we commit ourselves to the ongoing struggle of personal and social transformation. The kingdom of God with its vision of essential human dignity and common good is a far-reaching agenda with both seen and unseen implications. We do not know all it means. We are people of "this age," imbued with warped ideas of what makes for dignity and espousing what we consider credible purposes for the implicit and explicit violence of domination. We live with these mental voices that are reinforced by cultural assumptions and social structures. It is easy to comply with this mindlessly constructed world, especially when it is clear that any questioning or defection from the kingdoms of the earth will meet with ostracism. But praying "Thy kingdom come" sets us on a different path. It should not be said lightly.

Thy Will Be Done on Earth

The Hiding Earth

The earth is a place both where God is forgotten and where the dominant ways of sin alienate people from God and one another. More positively, it is also a place where heaven is not entirely missing. Rather it is hidden, buried in human situations and awaiting a moment of revelation and cooperation. This is fully in line with the relational consciousness of heaven because the Divine Reality who sustains the ones praying and all people, living and dead, also sustains all creation, including the earth. Therefore, when we carry the agenda of the beloved sons and daughters of our Father who art in heaven, we meet the agenda that heaven has a place in the earth, even though it is not immediately and clearly evident. It is as hidden as seeds.

The will of God (heaven) is like a seed implanted and active in the earth. Two short parables from the Gospel of Mark make this point:

> This is how it is with the kingdom of God; it is as if a man were to scatter seed on the land and would sleep and rise night and day and the seed would sprout and grow, he knows not how. Of its own accord the land yields fruit, first the blade, then the ear, then the full grain in the ear. And when the grain is ripe, he wields the sickle at once, for the harvest has come. (Mark 4:26-29)

A growth process is going on without human participation. The man is sleeping and rising; and while he is doing this, the earth is producing something by itself. It is hidden at first but it is becoming visible in stages. It develops through its own internal dynamics. The man will be a major actor for he has the sickle and will benefit from the harvest. But the seed is first and greater than the sickle:

> To what shall we compare the kingdom of God, or what parable can we use for it? It is like a mustard seed that, when it is sown in the ground, is the smallest of all the seeds on the earth. But once it is sown, it springs up and becomes the largest of plants and puts forth large branches, so that the birds of the sky can dwell in its shade. (Mark 4:30-32)

The seed is not only hidden, it is small. Commentaries often contrast the "smallness" of the seed with the "greatness" of its future and draw the comforting message of assurance. What is small today will one day be so great the "birds of the sky" (all nations) will find a home in its branches. But our emphasis is on development. Hidden is on its way to being seen; smallness is on its way to being large enough for all. This is how the will of God is at work in the conditions of the earth, and it is on the move.

Some characterize God's hidden and small will for human situations as a lure. It is present in each situation and searching for people and conditions that will actualize it. As Alfred North Whitehead said, people have an "intuition of immediate occasions as failing or succeeding in reference to the ideal relevant to them. There is a rightness attained or missed, with more or less completeness of attainment or omission."[13] Therefore, the situations of our lives are not neutral or just the raw material for our manipulative desires. There is hidden within them a possibility, a future that is emerging, a pregnancy that wants to be born. But it is not easy to discern the lure and assist in the birth.

Thy Will Be Done

The movement from the hiddenness of God's will to revealing it, from darkness to light, entails discernment. Elizabeth Barrett Browning's witty lines tell the tale:

> . . . Earth's crammed with heaven
> And every common bush afire with God:
> But only he who sees, takes off his shoes,
> The rest sit round it, and pluck blackberries . . . [14]

Earth is crammed with heaven, a permeating dimension of historical existence. The human role is not just to "bring heaven" into a place where it is missing. It is to actualize the present heaven to a greater degree onto the earth, and in the process get beyond "sit[ting] round and pluck[ing] blackberries."

Discerning God's will in creation as the inner drive to make situations all they can be can be a breakthrough realization. In his mythic autobiography *Report to Greco*, Nikos Kazantzakis recalls a time when his mind broke through to this elevating sense of the hidden will of God:

> I sat beneath the blossoming lemon tree in the courtyard, joyfully turning over in my mind a poem I had heard at Mount Athos: *"Sister Almond Tree, speak to me of God."* *And the almond tree blossomed.* . . .
>
> And as I thought this, my mind cleared. I realized that I had been seeking God all those years while never noticing that He was right in front of me, just like the fiancé who thinks he has lost his engagement ring, searches anxiously for it everywhere, and does not find it because he is wearing it on his finger. . . . Together with the birds and stars

> I yoked myself to the eternal wheel and for the first time in
> my life, I believe, felt what true liberty is: to place oneself
> beneath God's—in other words harmony's—yoke.[15]

The poem about the almond tree clears Kazantzakis's mind.
He sees he has always been engaged to God, but he did not
know it. The ring was on his finger, but he was looking elsewhere for it. Whatever else this God does, God blossoms all
that God inhabits.

Awakened by this realization, Kazantzakis knows he belongs with and to all creation, brother to the birds and the
stars. So he emulates in the conscious world this profound
sense of God's purpose that has been revealed to him. He
yokes himself to the eternal will and suddenly has a "feeling
understanding" of what true liberty is—to live an act in union
with God.

If Kazantzakis had a spiritual teacher/director, I suspect he
or she would encourage him to remember the gift of this realization. As this moment is succeeded by other moments and
different mental states, the truth he discerned might return to
hiddenness. His act of yoking himself to harmony with God
and creation might not endure through the rough-and-tumble
of unforeseen events. He might not be as confident that he
has the inner freedom that is necessary to be faithful to this
commitment. In order not to lose what he so values, he needs
to translate his experience of God whose presence brings creation and his own being into fulfillment into a practice. Praying
the Our Father might be a candidate.

Therefore, "Thy will be done" entails discerning the hidden force that seeks more and more influence in situations,
an influence that desires to bring the situation into all it can
be. Under the heading of "Befriending Life," Rachel Remen
has a profound insight into how we contribute to releasing
the hidden heaven onto the earth:

I've spent many years learning how to fix life, only to discover at the end of the day that life is not broken. There is a hidden seed of greater wholeness in everyone and everything. We serve life best when we water it and befriend it. When we listen before we act.

In befriending life, we do not make things happen according to our own design. We uncover something that is already happening in us and around us and create conditions that enable it. Everything is moving toward its place of wholeness. . . . It is always struggling against odds. Everything has a deep dream of itself and its fulfillment.[16]

A complementary step in the agenda of bringing heaven to earth is to listen to the dream of the earth itself in which heaven is already hidden. Situation after situation arises with a dream of its own fulfillment, its potential crying out to be actualized. It may be a dream and a potential that is "struggling against odds." But it is this dream and potential that connects heaven in creation with heaven in us; and, in doing so, discloses the path of our commitment and action.

When we pray "Thy will be done," we commit to the discipline of discernment. It is not an easy skill and it is not learned quickly. Alan Ecclestone saw it closely connected to the act of prayer, which "strives to penetrate through what to the eyes of un-engagement must be baffling and repellent, too hard to understand, too cruel to endure, too meaningless to use, in order to discern the lines of the emergent work, the future of Man being shaped, and in order to engage the one who prays with what is being wrought." I have often used this sentiment to center myself as I pray "Thy will be done." Whoever we ultimately are, there is an intuitive sense of rightness to want "to discern the line of the emergent work . . . and to yoke [ourselves] to what is being wrought."[17]

Deepening the Dare

The mission of the Lord's Prayer flows naturally from the identity the ones praying have dared to make their own. It deepens this dare because it announces what we dedicate ourselves to and makes known our concerns and commitments. To articulate this mission in the imagery of moving from heaven to earth suggests illumination plays a critical part. Heaven's sun brightens and makes visible the darkness of earth; rays of light shine to show us a way forward. Three paths come into view. They are not the only paths and these paths definitely lead to others. But in the prayer heaven is guidance and it throws light on where and how we are going to walk.

When we pray "hallowed be thy name," we know this commitment exists in the heaven-earth tension of remembrance and forgetfulness of the name of "Our Father who art in heaven." We cultivate a "remembering consciousness" of hallowing this name as the Mystery of Love, an intercommunion with Holy Being and with all other beings that permeates our comings and goings. This "remembering consciousness" strengthens our ability to see the Mystery of Love at work in us and in our situations. With our minds transformed by this commitment of the prayer, our spirits, grounded and informed by the Divine Spirit, will be released for our own fulfillment and the betterment of the earth.

When we pray "Thy kingdom come," we know this commitment exists in the heaven-earth tension of essential human dignity/common good and sinful domination. We cultivate a "change consciousness" that embraces both our individual and social realities. It challenges the behaviors and structures of sinful domination. We know we will suffer the consequences of those challenges. This "change consciousness" strengthens our ability to see both violations and positive examples of essential human dignity/common good in us, in others, and in social structures. With our minds transformed by this commitment of the prayer, our spirits, grounded and informed by the Divine Spirit, will be released for our own fulfillment and the betterment of the earth.

When we pray "Thy will be done," we know this commitment exists in the heaven-earth tension of discernment and hiddenness. We cultivate a "discernment consciousness" that we bring to situation after situation and in the process become aware of their dreams of fulfillment. This "discernment consciousness" strengthens our ability to see the will of God as a lure to excellence and fullness. With our minds transformed by this commitment of the prayer, our spirits, grounded and informed by the Divine Spirit, will be released for our own fulfillment and the betterment of the earth.

Although mission commitments ("hallowed be thy name. / Thy kingdom come. / Thy will be done on earth, as it is in heaven") deepen the dare of the identity, they are general orientations. Although some complain about this lack of specificity, it is an advantage. In general, mission orientations can become a context and influence in multiple situations. It maximizes their possible applications. What can appear abstract and detached is really the possibility of a widened outreach. However, out of all the possible ways these commitments could be enacted, the next and last section of the prayer focuses on three areas and three strategies within those areas that are particularly important.

CHAPTER 6

The Strategies of the Ones Praying

Our spiritual identity carries the heaven-driven mission of the name, kingdom, and will of our Father into the ways of the earth. These mission concerns are complemented by strategies that target specific areas and identify desired outcomes in those areas. The strategies in the Our Father focus on sustaining physical life ("Give us this day our daily bread"), reconciling social life ("forgive us our trespasses, as we forgive those who trespass against us"), and centering inner life ("lead us not into temptation, / but deliver us from evil"). Although there is not a strict correlation between the three mission orientations and the three strategies, they are interlocked, sharing perspectives and values. Mission and strategy inform and support one another, and, in doing so, they mobilize the ones praying.

We will explore and develop these strategies in the following sections:

- Giving Bread to Communicate Love
- Forgiving to Reconcile the Future

- Resisting to Center Inner Life
- Directing the Dare

The first three sections will focus on the spiritual motivations and dynamics that ground and inform these strategies. To do this, we will consult relevant spiritual teaching stories from the gospels. The final section will briefly indicate how the identity, mission, and strategies of the Our Father move into the day-in-day-out lives of the ones praying, how they direct the dare.

Giving Bread to Communicate Love

Today we need bread for we are hungry, but tomorrow we will still need bread because we will be hungry again. Today we need drink for we are thirsty, and we need clothing and shelter for without it we are naked and exposed to the elements. But tomorrow we shall need drink because thirst will return, and we will need clothing and shelter again for nakedness and exposure will return without them. The conditions of hunger, thirst, nakedness, and exposure do not go away with a single one-day response. These physical needs have to be met today and every day. "Give us *this day* our *daily* bread" is a statement that commits to the ongoing sustaining of physical life. What is needed this day is needed every day (daily). It is what the ones who are praying, congruent with their identity and mission, want to accomplish.

Breaking the Bread We Have

In Mark 6:31-44 there is a complex story that is usually called a feeding narrative. That description emphasizes the people who receive and eat the bread.

However, we will consider it as a spiritual teaching story about giving bread. Jesus is teaching his disciples how to give bread, how to share with others what they have, and discover a fuller meaning in this sharing. It illumines what "giving today our daily bread" means as a strategy that appears in a prayer that has previously established a spiritual identity and mission for the ones praying.[1]

A crowd pursues Jesus and his disciples into a place where they expected to be alone and have some rest. Even though Jesus' plans are interrupted, he does not send the crowd away. The story tells us his compassion takes him in another direction. He discerns the crowd is like "sheep without a shepherd," so he begins to teach them many things.

In Jesus' eyes to be "without a shepherd" is not to know something that is very important for well-being and flourishing. So Jesus, the Good Shepherd, will teach them what they need to know. However, as many times in the gospels, the teaching is not didactically spelled out in words but demonstrated in action. Also, although the crowd will benefit from the teaching, the targeted recipients are not the people but the disciples accompanying Jesus. They must be taught how to give bread to the people.

The first step in the teaching discloses and confronts the mindset of the disciples. The disciples tell Jesus how they analyze the crowd situation and what is the best thing to do. "This is a deserted place and it is already very late. Dismiss them so that they can go to the surrounding farms and villages and buy themselves something to eat" (Mark 6:35-36). This is a very commonsense strategy, but basically it is every person for oneself.

Also, it is not a strategy that fits Jesus' compassion. In a complementary story, Jesus spells out this compassion in detail: "My heart is moved with pity for the crowd, because they have been with me now for three days and have nothing to eat. If I send them away hungry to their homes, they will collapse on the way, and some of them have come a great distance" (Mark 8:2-3). Compassion, the ability to be with others and to see the world from their perspective, rejects the strategy of sending them away. Jesus has a different approach.

He tells the disciples, "You give them something to eat." But this direction is not immediately taken or accepted. Instead, the impossibility of doing what they think Jesus is suggesting is mocked: "Are we to go and buy two hundred denarii worth of bread, and give it to them to eat?" (6:37, NRSV). In short, their mind-set is: this is a deserted place and no food is available, so we would have to go somewhere where food is available, pay an exorbitant amount of money to buy that food, and then bring it back and give it to them. When the project is laid out that way, it is ludicrous.

But they have missed the meaning of Jesus' injunction, "You give them something to eat." For Jesus the key word is "you." So Jesus continues down his line of exploration and not the "mission impossible" scenario of the disciples. "How many loaves do you have? Go and see." The disciples find out they have "[f]ive loaves and two fish" (6:38). Although there is definitely an implied criticism that the disciples do not know what they have, the finding of seven (5+2) is meant to start a process of awakening in the reader, even if it may not do this in the disciples.

Although the story has stretched bread into the larger category of food that includes fish, the emphasis remains on seven. Seven is a number of wholeness and completion, the intersection of the spiritual and the physical. The story is moving from the disciples' constricted mind-set on large numbers that are unable to be met to a symbolic number that reminds them of their spiritual identity and mission. When Jesus instructs the people to recline on "the green grass" in that "deserted place," the story shifts further toward the spiritual. When grass grows in a place where the soil is not conducive, it means spiritual agency is at work.[2] The symbolic number and the green grass set the stage for the spiritual teaching about the meaning of giving physical food.

Jesus takes the five loaves and two fish, looks to heaven, and gives thanks. This indicates where Jesus is coming from, but not necessarily where the food is coming from. The food came from the provisions of the disciples. But it is in the hands of the one who comes from heaven, who knows himself as the beloved Son of the Father. It is he who will give the disciples' food back to them to distribute to the crowds. Jesus is trying to teach his disciples to give bread from an inner space of action that could be called "children of the Father." This is the consciousness we have inhabited by meditating on the first phrase, "Our Father who art in heaven."

Does that change the food? No, but it may change the motivation of the ones giving the food and the expectation of what the food will accomplish. Although the physical level of food is always to fill the stomach, another level reaches for a deeper satisfaction. In this story the emphasis is not merely sustaining physical life but on communicating love through sustaining physical life. These five loaves and two fish are carrying heaven's agenda onto the conditions of the earth.

In order for love to be communicated through the food, the ones who give the food have to give themselves through the food. It is not a matter of keeping one's distance while providing sustenance that is not us. We have to come with the food. In order to do that, we have to break ourselves and our resources in the process of giving. "Breaking" is the metaphor for self-giving. When that happens, the food becomes communion with the ones who are the beloved sons and daughters of our Father and brothers and sisters of all; and the people who eat it experience satisfaction, as the story carefully tells us. The "satisfaction" is the realization they have become what the ones giving them the bread know—they are the sons and daughters of Love and brothers and sisters of all. In this Mystery of Love there is no scarcity, as the disciples may have realized as they gathered up twelve baskets of leftovers. Twelve is the matching number of seven, enhancing the intersection of the spiritual and the physical with the character of abundance.

The purpose of giving bread is to relieve the hunger of people and communicate the Mystery of Love; the purpose of giving drink is to slake the thirst of people and communicate the Mystery of Love; the purpose of giving clothes is to cover the nakedness of people and communicate the Mystery of Love; and so on. All the corporal works of mercy are meant to comfort our physical vulnerabilities and, in the process, communicate the Mystery of Love. As we pray, "Give us this day our daily bread," we commit ourselves to personally and physically comforting all who are suffering diminishments and communicate to them the Mystery of Love that is never diminished.

Forgiving to Reconcile the Future

A case could be made that the dynamic interlocking of divine and human forgiveness is at the heart of the Lord's Prayer and of the Gospel itself, particularly the Gospel of Matthew. After the full rendition of the Lord's Prayer in the Sermon on the Mount, the forgiveness phrase is repeated at the end, and elaborated for emphasis: "If you forgive others their transgressions, your heavenly Father will forgive you. But if you do not forgive others, neither will your Father forgive your transgressions" (Matt 6:14-15). Also, after the parable of the forgiven yet unforgiving servant who the king consigns to debtor's prison, the lesson is made explicit: "So will my heavenly Father do to you, unless each of you forgives his brother from his heart" (Matt 18:35).

It is tempting to interpret this prayer phrase, its elaboration, and its parabolic gloss as a dire warning. What we do to one another determines what a heavier hitter (the heavenly Father) will do to us. Forgive and we will be forgiven; do not forgive and we will not be forgiven. We all know this dynamic of either violation and penalty or compliance and reward. With this interpretation, our motivation to heed this injunction is clearly self-interest. If we cannot comply out of internal conviction, comply out of fear of punishment.

However, a deeper analysis of the earth's condition and how heavenly consciousness and behavior should respond to it underlies this forgiveness scenario. The giving bread strategy presupposed the ongoing condition of hunger and so had to be employed daily. The forgiving strategy presupposes the ongoing breakdown of relationships and has to be employed continuously. There can be no letup in forgiveness because the fallback is revenge, retaliation, reprisal, and violence. Although we do ingenious and complex planning combined with calculating action to free ourselves from this habit of hatred, the gospels hold the unpopular conviction that the only way to break this chain reaction of attack breeding attack is forgiveness. As the giving bread story was a teaching for the disciples on how to give of themselves and their resources into the vulnerable lives of others to communicate love, the setup and story of the forgiven-unforgiving servant is a teaching for the disciples on how they should think about and act on forgiveness as the only way to find the freedom to create a reconciled future.[3]

No Other Way

The setup for the story of the forgiven yet unforgiving servant has Peter asking Jesus, "Lord, if my brother sins against me, how often must I forgive him?" (Matt 18:21). It appears to be a practical question. Peter envisions repeated offenses against him by a brother, a member of the Christian community. At the beginning he forgives the offender, as a follower of Jesus is enjoined to do. But this forgiveness is not met by effective repentance. The offender continues.

At this point, we might want to know more information that would be crucial to whether we are going to forgive. Is the offender malicious? Is he taking advantage of Peter's proneness to forgiveness? Or is he simply weak, unable to change? And what is the offense? Is it minor or is it major? Is this hurt deeply wounding to Peter or is it an irritant? However, this type of information, which common sense thinks is important, is not given. Peter may be asking a practical question, but the storyteller wants to make a deeper spiritual point.

Peter's question focuses on the limits of forgiveness. No matter what the offense is or who the person is, when can retaliation begin? At what number can Peter strike back? Peter seems to think seven might be the outside number. This is a quite generous estimate. Most people stop forgiving and start getting even at two. But the number seven is also a symbolic setup. It allows Jesus to use another number: "I say to you, not seven times but seventy-seven times" (18:22).

This wordplay recalls the boast of Lamech in Genesis: "I have killed a man for wounding me, / a young man for bruising me. / If Cain is avenged seven times, / then Lamech seventy-seven times" (Gen 4:23-24). The opposite of forgiveness is not a measured response in kind. It is escalated revenge. This is not the law of talons, an eye for an eye and a tooth for a tooth. It is an eye for a fingernail, a murder for a slap. Without forgiveness there is only increasing violence. In the following parable of the forgiven servant who is unforgiving to a fellow servant the breakdown of their relationship and the ensuing violence quickly follow on the failure of forgiveness.

However, Peter's question does not suck Jesus into a literal numbers game. Rather Jesus targets the foundational attitude of Peter. Peter is ready to retaliate. He just wants to know when. With this attitude forgiveness is a temporary, stalling strategy. If it works, fine. If it does not, there are other ways. This half commitment to forgiveness keeps people from investing their full creative potential into it. When the fallback is revenge, we may fall back too quickly. Jesus wants a full commitment to forgiveness as the only way, and with it a full use of our creative powers in the service of reconciliation. But with "paying back in kind" so normal a response, why should we be so unrelentingly committed to forgiveness?

Forgiveness and the Future

What is the reason for Jesus' hard line on forgiveness? As usual, Jesus uses a story to express and communicate what he sees with the hope that his vision will be communicated to those who hear the story:

> That is why the kingdom of heaven may be likened to a king who decided to settle accounts with his servants. When he began the accounting, a debtor was brought before him who owed him a huge amount. Since he had no way of paying it back, his master ordered him to be sold, along with his wife, his children, and all his property, in payment of the debt. At that, the servant fell down, did him homage, and said, "Be patient with me, and I will pay you back in full." Moved with compassion the master of that servant let him go and forgave him the loan. (Matt 18:23-27)

This is a symbolic story in its basic structure but not in all its details. It begins by portraying the relationship between God (the king) and a sinner (the servant) who is mercifully forgiven. The story opens with an accounting, a revelation of debt, and a judgment that destroys the life of the servant and his family. (Most probably, the original meaning of debt was literally money. As the tradition developed, debt moved to general trespassing and eventually settled into sin.) The servant has made a "huge" mistake, a mistake that is found out and cannot be repaid. This mistake will put him and his family in bondage forever.

Since the sinful servant is about to lose everything, he will promise anything. He pleads with the king in the only categories available to him, the conditions of strict justice. He wants more time in order to repay. However, even if this is granted, his life continues to be dominated by his mistake. The amount is so huge he will be forever in debt. Any way the king decides, the rest of his life will be equated with his mistake and burdened by it. There is no way justice can save him. He may be on his knees before the king, but his back is against the wall.

Suddenly compassion enters, and it releases a flow of mercy in the king. This flow of mercy is what some Christian theologies consider the essence of the Divine. The human condition is mired in sin and is not able to extricate itself by its own efforts. It needs mercy. But the depth of deprivation does not cause mercy. The mercy comes from the heart of God. It is grace, a free response of God arising out of divine compassion for the servant beneath the sinner, for the person beneath his imponderable debt.

Therefore, in the story the mercy comes as a shock. Nothing the king or the man have previously done prepares for it. It comes out of the future, not as a logical extension of the past. When it arrives, it changes everything. The man is both released from bondage and forgiven his debt. What previously dominated and threatened his life and the life of his family is no longer present. In his case, the slogan is accurate: this is the first day of the rest of his life. He is a characterization of the classic Christian category—a forgiven sinner.

This story has family resemblances to the story of the prodigal son we rehearsed in chapter 4. In that story the compassion of the Father will not allow the self-hating script of the prodigal son to define him and dictate his future. He insists on affirming the Son beneath the prodigal. In this story the compassion of the King refuses to leave the indebted servant and his family to their fate, the terrible fate of a total life of indentured service. His forgiveness propels a new reality, a future that was not possible before the advent of compassion. He affirms the true servant beneath the debtor of wrong deeds. The prodigal son and the forgiven servant reflect a similar underlying experience, the refusal to allow mistakes to rule the future; and the only way that can happen is the arrival of forgiveness. Forgiveness is more concerned about the future than the past.

Not Forgiving Ends Receiving

However, the forgiven servant story takes us further than the prodigal son story. We are not told how the prodigal son received his restoration into sonship. But we are told what the forgiven servant does with his forgiveness. He goes out and finds a fellow servant who owes him a paltry amount compared to what he owed the king. This fellow servant says the same thing to him as he said to the king. But the forgiven servant cannot love his neighbor as himself. Instead of forgiveness, he throttles his fellow servant and sends him off to debtor's prison.

Then a startling thing happens: "Then in anger his master handed him over to the torturers until he should pay back the whole debt" (Matt 18:34). The king's mercy dries up. It recedes back into him, so to speak. This leaves the man to the consequences of his original mistake. Divine mercy may be freely given. But if it is not imitated and given away, it ceases to be effective in the lives of those who have received it. Divine forgiveness and inter-human forgiveness are tightly linked. They are connected through the heart, the spiritual center of the person.

This is the lesson Matthew makes explicit: "So will my heavenly Father do to you, unless each of you forgives his brother from his heart" (18:35). The heart, as we saw in chapter 4, is the symbolic place that connects heaven and earth, opens to both God and neighbor. It receives forgiveness from God and extends that forgiveness to others. If it fails to extend forgiveness to others, it loses the forgiveness it has received from God. The human non-forgiveness rescinds God's forgiveness. This is not because Divine Reality has changed its mind but because another spiritual law has become operative. The measure we measure is measured unto us.

So this is what Jesus is saying to Peter, who wants to know when he can strike back: "You live by the forgiveness of God. You must never forget that. That is your identity-forming experience. It is *this* experience, and not the experience of being wronged, that you always 'repay in kind.' The more you extend that experience to others, the more you grow in its mercy. However, the failure to do this means the forgiveness recedes. You are returned to a life of bondage to the consequences of your huge sin. If you understand this truth, you will not ask, 'How many times?'"

Finding New Life

The phrase "forgive us our trespasses, as we forgive those who trespass against us" supported by the spiritual teaching story of the forgiven-unforgiving servant invites us into a complex psychological-spiritual strategy. God's forgiveness begins a process that may or may not be developed. It is developed if the one forgiven forgives another. Then there is in effect a forgiveness chain; and we assume the newly forgiven one will recognize his forgiveness is not the largesse of one person but is mediated by the forgiveness of God. This realization facilitates extending the forgiveness they have received to someone else.

But there is a doubling back in this process of moving forward. As we forgive others, we enter more deeply into the forgiveness of God. To use the categories of chapter 3, when we integrate forgiveness into our interpersonal relationships and social structures, we strengthen our realization of its truthfulness, our understanding of its psychological and social dynamics, and become more authentically committed to the faith that grounds and generates the whole process. Passing forgiveness along is a form of growth in the original forgiveness.

Why is there this emphasis on an ultimate forgiveness scenario in which humans are immersed and which is initiated and energized by the Source of life itself? Because without our ability to receive God's forgiveness and grow in it, the interpersonal and social processes that are energized by the breakdown of relationships and the consequent reprisals are too formidable and overwhelming to be taken on and successfully resolved. We all know family and friendships that have broken down and will never be rebuilt. We all can cite ethnic and national rivalries that perdure through generations, even centuries. Joy Williams, in *Ninety-Nine Stories of God*, tells this vignette:

> In the 1973 Yom Kippur War, Israel was poised to launch nuclear warheads—the Temple Weapons—rather than suffer defeat at the hands of the Arabs. At the time, Israel

had at least thirteen twenty-kiloton atomic bombs—the Hiroshima bomb was sixteen kilotons. Armageddon was avoided only when the U.S. Secretary of State, Henry Kissinger, acting in the vacuum left by the travails of his "drunken friend," President Richard Nixon, authorized an emergency resupply of high-tech, though conventional, weaponry to the Israelis.

Prime Minister Golda Meir said:

"We can forgive the Arabs for killing our children. We cannot forgive them for forcing us to kill their children."[4]

We sense forgiveness is the only way. But we doubt our ability to pull it off and the ability of our enemies to receive it.

This persuasiveness of human estrangement and the acceptance of the course of retaliation forces a new perspective on forgiveness. First, we have to acknowledge our bondage. We often overlook the fact that sinful experiences have the power to claim us. The experiences of both being sinned against and sinning are seldom over and done with. They continue to extend their influence long after the actual offense has ended. The "huge amount" of the servant's debt may symbolize sin's power to dominate us and bring our future under its control. Negative experiences infiltrate our mind and heart and constrict our freedom. They become the bondage and prison the servants in the story experience, a bondage and a prison from which they cannot free themselves.

Second, the desire to bring forgiveness into situations against overwhelming odds can be strengthened by recognizing forgiveness equates to new and reconciled life. Forgiveness is not primarily overlooking past sinfulness or, in the metaphor of the story, canceling past debt. Rather "forgiveness" in many situations is exactly what Jesus intimated—the only way. It is about life or death. Therefore, the ones who bring forgiveness must project an intense giving of life and energy into the freedom of a person or a people on the edge of newness. This giving must be creative and concentrated because the weight of past negative experiences is great.

In this context, Beatrice Bruteau compares the human person to a "coral."[5] When we think of coral, we usually think of a "pinkish stone that is found in the reefs or on beaches and can be polished and set into jewelry." But the biologist sees something different. The coral is really a polyp, a little animal that leaves behind the stony mass that was its skeleton and moves forward to continue to interact with its environment. The emphasis is not what it was but what it is in the continual journey of its becoming. This is the essence of forgiveness. It does not focus on the "remains," on the past that is no longer in the present. Rather it is an intense giving into the emerging person who is seeking new life.

Third, in these recalcitrant estrangements we will need courageous initiatives, better strategies, and convincing and adaptable tactics. But we will also need to maximize the desire for new life and allow its powerful call to be heard in our hearts. As we go forward, we can go back to our own primordial forgiveness, knowing we are not a pristine solution but an essential part of the problem, a forgiven sinner looking for a way to pass on new life to others who we perceive more and more clearly want new life for themselves. The unlikely suggestion of the forgiveness phrase of the Our Father and its supporting spiritual teaching story is to return to your original freedom beyond the debt you incurred.

The Receiver of Mercy

With this intention, it is worthwhile asking a question the spiritual teaching story does not consider. When the other servants see what the unforgiving behavior of the forgiven servant does, they squeal to the king. The king calls in the servant whom he had forgiven: "You wicked servant! I forgave you your entire debt . . . Should you not have had pity on your fellow servant, as I had pity on you?" (Matt 18:32-33). Everyone seems to "get it" but the forgiven servant. The king and the other servants know the burden of being forgiving is to forgive others. Why didn't the forgiven-unforgiving servant get this "pay it forward" connection?

The parable doesn't tell us, but we can guess. Perhaps the forgiven servant took his forgiveness lightly. He thought he got lucky. Or he flattered himself into thinking he perfectly played his pleading to the soft side of the king. Then, getting what he wanted, he promptly forgot the whole thing. He went about his business with the usual knee-jerk reaction of "pay me back or I will punish you."

Without memory and internalization, our positive experiences do not produce the positive result of passing them on to others. The gospel imperative of "freely receiving, freely giving" is short-circuited (see Matt 10:8). We have freely received, and then we have promptly freely forgotten. It is not enough to have the experience. We must work with the experience to allow it to change our minds and behavior:

- Remember a time we were forgiven.
- Host this time in our minds and hearts.
- Ponder what it taught us.
- Be grateful to the people who were involved.
- Be on the lookout to give as we have received.

Just as those who gave bread had to give the bread they had, those who forgive have to give the forgiveness they have. In the Our Father it is the acting person who is always the focus.

This grounding experience of forgiveness, in the freshness of a new life we did not create, is the space where our consciousness must rest. We must not bolt out of our prison without understanding or appreciation and go on with life exactly as before. We must allow what has happened to form and influence us. If we do not deeply grasp both the bondage to our mistakes and the unmerited forgiveness, we will not persist in the freedom and the future we have been given.

We walk into an open future that is not the result of anything we did. So we cannot claim it. The usual way we differentiate ourselves from others is not operative. It is not our merit that has forced the forgiveness, or even our potential for more service that has rendered forgiveness a reasonable choice. We might try to attribute the forgiveness to dumb luck. We got the king on a good day. But the depth of what we have experienced will finally penetrate. A future, free from the consequences of our mistakes, was bestowed upon us.

The implications of this graceful experience come into view when we meet our former selves in others. We gradually realize *our* situation is *the* situation. All of us are tied to our past failures until a future is bestowed upon us. These failures may be small, but they hamper freedom. They imprison people. Since we were given a way out, we know the way out. Only now we are on the other side. Our hope is to clearly remember the conditions of our liberation. If we forget them, we will return to bondage. This will happen long before we are reported to the king. It happens the moment we put our hands around the throat of our debtor. We are once again sold into the slavery of revenge, retaliation, and reprisal. As difficult as it is and as resistant as we are to it, the only way forward is "forgive us our trespasses, as we forgive those who trespass against us." The prayer calls us to the freedom of a reconciled future.

Resisting to Center Inner Life

"[L]ead us not into temptation, / but deliver us from evil" is realistic about the power of temptations and evil to carry us into thoughts and actions that contradict our true identity as the sons and daughters of our Father. As the ancient phrase suggests, "The devil goes about as a roaring lion seeking whom he may devour." In a world this dangerous, the street-wisdom is surely correct: "Unless you are prepared not to, you will." Therefore, there is a paradoxical character to the last strategy. The last strategy is to resist false strategies that consistently and attractively come our way. But this is more than just an adamant "no" to what contradicts spiritual identity. This resistance creates an emptiness that allows love to emerge as a steady, strong alternative. We may discover the truth about ourselves by resisting the falsehoods that parade as the way we should think and act.

There are two gospel stories that directly connect to "lead us not into temptation, / but deliver us from evil." The first is the temptation narratives in the Synoptic Gospels (Matt 4:1-11; Mark 1:12-13; Luke 4:1-13).[6] In Mark, these temptations are just mentioned, but in Matthew and Luke they are spelled out in illuminating detail. However, it is the introduction that connects them to this final phrase of the Our Father. After Jesus' baptism, the Spirit immediately leads him into the desert to be tempted by Satan. The identity of the baptism needs to undergo scrutiny. This identity may unfold into mission, but it also attracts temptations. In fact, for many the temptations may come first and navigating them is the way to find the mission. If it was that way with the Lord in the desert, might it be that way with those who pray the Lord's Prayer?

The second story is the Gethsemane episode (Luke 22:39-53). Although in the temptation narratives Satan's strategies are convincingly rejected, he is not defeated. "[Satan] departed from him until an opportune time" (Luke 4:13, NRSV). Strategies that contradict our spiritual identity are always part of our life. "Opportune times" are every time we are faced with decisions and actions. This happens on the eve of Jesus' passion and death and, once again, it is a teaching moment for the disciples. The lesson is clearly stated twice as Jesus commands his disciples, "Pray, lest you enter into temptation." Although they will not be able to do this, we will see Jesus do it as, perhaps surprisingly, he prays his own prayer. The last phrase of the Lord's Prayer alludes to a time when the Lord himself prays the prayer he gave us. In the imagery of the episode, it is his path of staying awake and having the strength not to succumb to temptation and do evil.[7] Could there be a better way to end our prayer than by joining with Jesus in the same prayer and, in the process, reinforcing our commitment to its practice?

Tempting Beloved Sons and Daughters

Jesus' baptismal identity as the beloved Son immediately leads to the temptations. They are Spirit guided and intrinsic to the process of claiming his identity. Although they are dangerous because they could compromise his identity and take it down a wrong path, they can also purge the identity of false understandings and false strategies. Breakthrough moments like a voice of loving assurance from heaven seldom come with a complete set of instructions. The path has to be discovered in the aftermath.

These temptations take place in the desert, the traditional place where the meaning of deeper experiences is clarified. Satan is the one who proposes the temptations. His suggestions to Jesus are meant to subvert God's plans. They present themselves as strategic implications of being the beloved Son of God. But they are not. Since Jesus successfully resists these action plans, the temptations turn into a "testing of the heart" and work to deepen his sense of sonship. Indeed, after the temptations Jesus "returned . . . in the power of the Spirit" (Luke 4:14). What was meant to undermine has strengthened.

One of the conclusions of the Matthean/Lukan temptation narratives is that being the beloved Son of the voice from the heavens is not a privilege that confers physical, social, and religious exemptions and benefits. In the first temptation, Jesus resists using miraculous powers to feed himself by turning rocks into bread. Although Jesus is concerned about giving people bread, that feeding is about communicating love to physical needs. It is not about reducing human existence to physical needs and meeting them for our own benefit while others starve. As such, he refutes Satan by claiming living is about "every word that comes forth from the mouth of God." The spiritual truth of food includes the food itself but goes beyond it.

In the third temptation in Luke and the second in Matthew, Satan suggests floating down from the pinnacle of the temple. This spectacular feat will gain Jesus notoriety and adulation. Although it will be an external credential that his teaching is correct, it will take attention away from the internal dynamics of the teaching. It will also fall into the trap of "testing theology," putting yourself in a dangerous situation and asking God to save you as a sign of special claims. This sick approach is summed up as "tempting God." Satan begins both these false strategies with "If you are the Son of God." Jesus resists them by bringing forward the true nature of the Son of God.

While we can smile at these temptations and say tongue in cheek that neither of these options is within our powers, the seduction to make ourselves the center of everything is always attractive. This self-centered absorption that Satan suggests goes against the relational individuality of our true identity. But there are deep-seated tendencies that can hijack the equality of sons and daughters of our Father and make it a special identity that gives us the edge we need. Our shaky egos are always in need of bolstering and what could be better than a voice from heaven? So when Satan suggests strategies of specialness, they seem perfectly appropriate. After all, we are the beloved sons and daughters of our Father. It should be worth something. It is no use being special if we cannot make it work for us. In other words, the voice from heaven can enter into the chorus of earthly voices that drown out its distinctiveness and turn it into an asset in the project of what the gospels call "being first."

But the most intriguing of the temptations is the offer to give Jesus what belongs to Satan—the kingdoms of the earth. Satan shows Jesus these kingdoms in a single instant, revealing the inner dynamics that make them work. Their essence is captured in the tempter's name. Satan, "Satanas," means the accuser and devil, "diabolus," means the one who tears things apart, the divider. The kingdoms of the world work by the strategies of accusation and division. If we want to advance in these kingdoms, these ploys will prove valuable. Worshiping Satan is the path of success.

But Jesus is already committed to another strategy. His identity is tied to receiving divine love and, therefore, he is moving in the way of communicating that love and making possible forgiveness and reconciliation. Once again, Jesus will bring about the kingdom not by the reigning tactics of temporal power but by the personal call to conversion. Forgive one another and be reconciled is the way forward. This path is not found in the kingdoms of the world. They are not to be imitated: they are to be transformed.

Jesus may be conscious of his true identity in a clear and immediate way. Therefore, he is portrayed as a strength and directness more forceful than Satan's deviousness. But for most of us holding fast to our identity as beloved sons and daughters of our Father and brothers and sisters of all is a more labored and scrutinizing effort. We are not always centered on our spiritual identity. So temptations appear to us as options, possibilities that have to be weighed rather than demonic misdirections that have to be dismissed. In particular, temptations are attractive because they appeal to our fantasy selves, those aspects of ourselves that want to be above it all. They arrive as lucky opportunities, our good fortune to have what we always wanted—a life that is always satiated, without injury, and rippling with splendiferous power. How can we remember who we are when we are offered this tantalizing possibility of fantasies we have always entertained? The answer in the teaching story of Gethsemane is to do what we have been proposing—to pray the Our Father as a transformative spiritual practice.

Praying and Temptation

The Gethsemane story has the same purpose as the giving bread story in Mark and the forgiving and unforgiving servant in Matthew. All three are carefully crafted spiritual teaching stories for discipleship. At the beginning of the Gethsemane story Jesus states unequivocally the lesson the disciples are to learn: "Pray, lest you enter into temptation" (Luke 22:40). The implication is that if we do not pray, temptation will overwhelm or capture us, making us victims of its negative attraction. As such, prayer is the preparation for action; and the action, at least in the first moment, includes rigorous and sustained resistance.

Temptation and resistance can be understood in the spiritual categories of inner and outer, the same categories we employed to understand the movement from heaven to earth. The outer world is always soliciting us to act on its terms. These terms may be good or bad, but when we categorize them as temptation, we evaluate them as bad. They want us to participate in them according to their negative dynamics. They have a purpose and a direction, and they will pull us along unless we have the strength to resist. The strength to resist comes from prayer. When we pray to the Father who is eager to give, we establish an inner spiritual power that has the ability to push back. It provides the ability not only to say "no" but to forge a new and unforeseen "yes." The Spirit whom the Father is eager to give heightens our positive power to enact God's will. This is the lesson the disciples are meant to learn. However, it will be a painful lesson, deeply realized in their failure to enact it.

But it is a lesson Jesus exemplifies. He kneels upon the earth and prays, "Father, if you are willing, take this cup away from me; still, not my will but yours be done" (Luke 22:42). This is a gloss on "Thy will be done." It is the brief accompanying language that interprets the phrase and connects it to the specific situation that is unfolding. The human, heartfelt side of those words is their focus on the conflict of wills between Jesus and his Father. Jesus looks ahead and sees the inevitable clash between himself and the religious and political authorities; and he knows the way these powerful forces deal with their irritations. He does not want to suffer, and he prays to God not to let this happen. Surely, this is the prayer of everyone looking into a future of possible pain and death. There is no glory in suffering, and no one should seek it.

But Jesus loves something more than he fears suffering. He is thoroughly committed to the divine will. However, God's will is not that Jesus suffers and dies. God's will is that the invitation to forgiveness and reconciliation be continued in all circumstances. This is what Jesus has pledged to do. In the events that will unfold, Jesus will remain steadfast to that commitment. He will never succumb to the violence of the outer world when it seeks to have him imitate it. He will forgive his persecutors (Luke 23:34) and offer paradise to the repentant thief (Luke 23:43). His ability to do this is because of his prayer life, a life that keeps him aware of God as the spiritual center from whom his actions flow. In our terms, he translates prayer time into daytime.

However, access to this spiritual center and persevering in its energy is difficult. In response to Jesus' prayer, an angel is sent who, in a way analogous to masseuses who prepare athletes to compete in the games, assists Jesus in his prayer. Masseuses work the bodies of athletes until they are ready for the contests ahead. The athletes sweat water, but Jesus sweats blood. This symbol portends the approaching violence. Jesus' praying is not seeking help in making the right decision. This praying is about strengthening the will. This is why he is in agony. His prayer demands earnestness, a strenuous increase of attention and commitment. He is about to enter a contest and strength, the steady and unrelenting flow of love, is needed.

But the strength that Jesus finds in prayer will not be found in his disciples. They have not stayed awake. This means more than they have physically fallen asleep. It means they have not stayed in communion with their spiritual center through the act of praying. Their inability to do this is because they "sleep from sorrow." "Sleeping from sorrow" is a condition that judges the circumstances they will face to be far greater than the resources they are able to muster. So they shrink, pull back from engagement, lay down their arms, and surrender. Quite simply, they are overwhelmed and overcome. The world is too much for them.

What Jesus says to them is literally meant as a wake-up call. "Why do you sleep?" is a prophetic question that disturbs the slumber of the disciples. In some ways the question is unanswerable in language. Jesus is not asking them to explain themselves, to give a reason for their failure to heed his advice at the beginning of the episode. Any verbal response would smack of rationalization and excuse. The only response is renewed action, and Jesus tells them what the action is: "Rise and pray, lest you enter into temptation."

Therefore, the injunction to pray as a way to avoid temptation begins and ends this episode. Readers cannot miss the message. But the disciples who did miss the message will now demonstrate what happens to those who fall asleep. They have not listened to Jesus; they have not prayed to the Father who was willing to give them the Spirit; and they will not resist temptation. They will give into violence and abandon Jesus.

But Jesus will not. He will confront Judas's betrayal but he will not betray Judas; he will heal the violence of his disciples' sword-wielding but he will not wield the sword; he will expose the lies of the chief priests, elders, and temple police but he will not lie. He resists all three temptations, but he does so from his identity as Son of God. He does not enter them in such a way that he conforms to their negative energies, becoming betrayal, violence, and lies in order to resist them. He is not "led into temptation." His prayer time has become the vehicle that facilitates "delivering him from evil."

Directing the Dare

The Our Father ends without an ending. There is no "Amen." "Amen" connotes our hope that what the prayer has been about will be realized. "Let it be so!" Although this hope is an under-current of the whole prayer, saying "Amen" can have the side effect of moving the ones praying from their own commitment and engagement in the prayer's projects to a vague sense that this may somehow come about without their concentrated efforts. The "somehow" often translates into God providing providential occurrences. Although graced and unforeseen events may happen, we should not depend on them as a sub-stitute for our own creativity. Instead the ending that is not an ending urges the ones praying to "rise from prayer" (as Jesus did in Gethsemane) and move into the challenges of the day, directing the dare into the world they encounter. The prayer is not over; it is simply moving.

The last strategy, "lead us not into temptation, / but deliver us from evil," helps this transition. It readies the ones praying for what they will certainly meet during the day. The day is not eagerly waiting for them with their prayer-formed consciousness. The day is already in full gear, its temptations disguised and inviting and its opportunities to do evil well-established and respectable. The consciousness that the prayer time cultivated can be quickly forgotten and/or overwhelmed by the rush of events. When this happens, the protocol is succinct: return to the prayer and then return to the day.

What the day demands as it unfolds is tactics and centering. Both of which are moveable feasts. Tactics take account of the concrete particularities of situations, identify obstacles and opportunities, decide the sequence of actions, devise changes as "things" develop one way or another, and so on. They include both planning and adaptability, having an agenda and "calling an audible." Praying prepares the person to act, but it cannot envision the action or perform it. It directs the dare, but it does not carry it out. Praying the Our Father as a transformative spiritual practice translates into entering a tactical world of perseverance and revision.

Centering complements tactics and says, "It is important what you do, but it is equally important from 'where' you do it." In spiritual traditions, the person has to be properly disposed in order for the action to be effective. "Where" actions come from complements "what" the actions are. Praying has opened consciousness to an effective "where," a deeper center of love. Once we have experienced it on a regular basis, we know where it is—so to speak. When we are in other states of consciousness, we can return to the "son and daughter of love" consciousness and, dwelling there, speak and act. In this way, we bring the prayer consciousness into whatever tactics we are using to engage the situation. In short, as tactics have to evaluated and revised, the center can be lost and will have to be regained.

The truth is, none of us knows where the prayer may take us. If it becomes the consulting companion of our lives, it may haunt our judgments and shadow our decisions. Common sense may take a beating, and we might hesitate to endorse and pursue the highly regarded cultural indicators of success. There is good reason to suspect the prayer may introduce us into sacrifices and conflicts that will make us uneasy. Sacrifices and conflicts marked the life of the one who gave it to us. It is unlikely his inheritance will have lost that character. In short, the prayer may have its way with us. Engaging its dare also includes accepting it as a mysterious adventure.

But as we walk with the prayer, we may find a strange combination of humility and importance developing in us. This is not a humility that has a secret pride at its center, preening as a meritorious virtue. Rather it has the stubbornness, even coldness, of a metaphysical fact. We are either mediums of a greater, more inclusive, and mysteriously loving Reality or we are out on our own, dashing and dueling with the time given. The prayer opts for a medium identity, mission, and strategy. When this truth is fully internalized, we may find ourselves both relaxed and energized, restful with never knowing the whole of it and at the same time eager for the next possibility. Our thinking and actions better or worsen the world. But they do not make us competitively important, dividing us from others and assuring our specialness. We are merely trying, as best as our wits allow, to give expression to who we really are as the sons and daughters of our Father and brothers and sisters of all. And, if St. Paul is correct and "Love never ends" (1 Cor 13:8), then neither does the dare nor the adventure.

CHAPTER 7

Transformations and the Emergence of Spirit

This final chapter summarizes the seven transformations we are invited into when we pray the Our Father. Through these transformations Spirit is released into our minds and bodies and elevates our interpersonal and social interactions. The previous chapters have explored this vision in detail, but the language of this summary contrasts the "before and after" of the transformations and envisions the emerging Spirit as a homecoming.

Seven Transformations

As we pray the Our Father, we are invited into seven transformations. Each transformation consists in a *move from* some way of thinking, willing, feeling, and acting to a *move to* another way of thinking, feeling, and acting. The mind of the prayer has a highly developed psycho-spiritual consciousness; and as we encounter it, our conventional consciousness, often submerged and taken for granted, is brought out of hiding and challenged. Although at times the call of this transformative process can seem like a command, it is really an invitation. As all invitations, it solicits our freedom and brings us to the edge of decision. We can either ignore or pursue the transformation.

If we pursue the transformation, the seven challenges of transformative spiritual practices in general will come into play in a way that corresponds to the complexities of our individual histories. We will struggle with resistance, gradualness, integration, desire, expectations, perseverance, and attention. Also, the seven challenges that are distinctive to the Our Father will emerge, most likely not all at once but in a serendipity that relates to our mental processes. We will have to explicitly assent to the project of putting on the *mind* of Christ, translate the symbolic language into relevant meanings, cooperate with the structure of the prayer as religious motivation for social action, interpret petition language as a way of human openness rather than as a way of asking for divine intervention, live comfortably on the continuum of faith, understanding, and realization, experiment with integrating behaviors into our daily life that are consistent with the prayer, and pause to sync our mouths with our minds as we pray the words. These challenges bring us a step at a time into a revelation of who we are, becoming followers of the one who taught us to pray this way.

The first transformation, "Our Father who art in heaven," is the most daunting, requiring a far-reaching reconception of our identity. But it is also the foundational consciousness for the entire prayer. Its background is understanding ourselves as dimensional beings—spiritual, psychological, physical, social, and cosmic—with each dimension an essentially relational reality. We are never separate, isolated entities defined and buffeted by "the winds that blow." Our individuality and uniqueness emerge out of and are always sustained by a formative relational mix. However, it is difficult to hold fast to this truth.

Therefore, the first transformation is a *move from* the habitual inclination to describe ourselves as a combination of discrete elements of our physical, psychological, or social dimensions. The *move to* is to determine and coincide with our ultimate spiritual identity. The relationality of the spiritual dimension is the most thoroughgoing and enters into and influences the other dimensions. As spiritual beings, we are receiving life and love at every moment from the immanent-transcendent Mystery that sustains and calls forward us, all other people, both the living and the dead, and all creation. This reality is Our Father who art in heaven. When we say these words, each of us explicitly is one of the beloved sons and daughters of our Father and brothers and sisters of all.

The second transformation, "hallowed be thy name," is a *move from* forgetting this identity of our Father who art in heaven as we immerse ourselves in the urgent and demanding projects of the physical and social survival on the earth. It is a *move to* hallowing the name of our Father who art in heaven through remembering the Mystery of Love in the throes of all our struggles and trusting in that Mystery even when the evidence against it is overwhelming.

The third transformation, "Thy kingdom come," is to *move from* conforming to the cultural systems in which we live (kingdoms of the earth), which shape our behaviors, and position us within structures that legitimate the sinful domination of the many by the few. It is a *move to* challenge ourselves and these earth kingdoms to extend universal human dignity and develop greater common good participation in the benefits of earth and society. There will be a cost to this movement that pushes against the inertia of our present ways; it will be the cross we bear. But this cost is not merely a regrettable result. The way we bear it is the heart of the transformation itself and the power of its attraction.

The fourth transformation, "Thy will be done," is to *move from* watching situation after situation unfold in terms of its inherent and often negative circumstances and not suspecting a deeper dynamic is calling to our initiative and creativity. The *move to* is to discern the hidden lures in those situations to make them all they can be and focus our freedom to cooperate with this will of our Father who art in heaven.

The fifth transformation, "Give us this day our daily bread," is to *move from* the exclusive priority of sustaining our own vulnerable physical lives and to be indifferent to the vulnerable physical lives of others. The *move to* is to recognize and respond to the hunger, thirst, nakedness, homelessness, sickness, and dying of all as a way to communicate the love of beloved sons and daughters of our Father and brothers and sisters of all.

The sixth transformation, "forgive us our trespasses, as we forgive those who trespass against us," is to *move from* our ingrained compulsion for retaliation and reprisal that is always legitimated by powerful innate compulsions and convincing conceptual arguments. The *move to* is a call to center ourselves in the truth of our own forgiveness as the energy of forgiving others, finding new life, and reconciling the future.

The seventh transformation, "lead us not into temptation, / but deliver us from evil," is to *move from* thinking and acting as if our spiritual identity conferred privilege and exemption from life's difficulties and gave us access to the powers of the earth on their own terms, engaging situations with strategies of betrayal, violence, and lies. The *move to* is to examine our spiritual identity to resist our self-serving interests and pray the Lord's Prayer to gain the strength to carry out the values of our identity in situations that are hostile to them.

The Emergence of Spirit

When these transformations are articulated in this way, they are skeletal sketches. They can appear dangerously abstract and pathetically ideal, one more exercise in human pie-in-the-sky. But if we take on the practice, the strong desires and tenuous decisions of each day provide the flesh and blood of these transformations.

On one level, the resulting struggles defy prediction. The transformed mind is a newly formed mind and what it will see, will, feel, and do in the world is not given with the change. Once the practice puts us on the path, we take our chances. However, on another level, we share Paul's stubborn consolation: "For if we live, we live for the Lord, and if we die, we die for the Lord; so then, whether we live or die, we are the Lord's" (Rom 14:8). We realize this "bottom line" is what we have been about from the beginning.

However, as we engage these transformations—small or large, trivial or important—something may happen that generated Paul's cry of "Abba! Father!" and most likely was the purpose Jesus shared this discipleship prayer with us. Spirit may emerge because the tight and clever ways our minds have blocked Spirit have been loosened. I have always been impressed by the Christian reticence in Spirit talk. We talk about gifts of the Spirit and the fruits of the Spirit.[1] We focus on the effects on persons and situations and not on direct, unmediated encounter. When Spirit is present, certain things happen in our cognitive-affective sensibilities and in our interpersonal and social interactions. The word that is often used is our faculties are "elevated."[2] In other words, they are made excellent and become increasingly committed to the service for which they were made.

Of course, Spirit is always present, a given of human existence. The imagery from the book of Revelation lays it out:

"Behold, I stand at the door and knock. If anyone hears my voice and opens the door, [then] I will enter his house and dine with him, and he with me" (Rev 3:20). The Lord is always knocking. He is not a come-and-go visitor; he forever waits at the door. Praying the Lord's Prayer is hearing his voice as he knocks and opening the door is entering into the transformative process. As we all know, eating with Jesus is more than a physical act. It is his Spirit entering into us through the food.

As the transformations open the door to the Spirit, what will happen? How will our faculties be elevated? Tradition says our minds will be illumined, our wills will be inspired, and our hearts will be gladdened. Our illumined minds will see and become convinced of the relational structure of the human and cosmic worlds grounded in the self-giving of God. Our inspired wills will be driven to live out the transformations into which the prayer invites us. It will gradually dawn on us that Spirit has been behind and through the practice from the beginning. But we only came to know it as we developed to a certain point. This illumination and inspiration translates into creativity and perseverance. These are the virtues, the steady powers needed to bring heaven to earth.

Most poignantly, our hearts will be gladdened. As the transformations affect our thinking, feeling, and acting, there will be a surge of passion, pleasure, and purpose in who we are and how we are living. The blahness of what T. S. Eliot called "Living and partly living" will fade.[3] We will develop an ability to integrate negative circumstances and unforeseeable twists. The Spirit has empowered our capacity to transcend and include whatever happens. We will be alive in a way that does not pump our ego, but humbles us into our soul where we rest in the communion of God, neighbor, and earth supported by the bonds and flow of love. The transformative spiritual practice of praying the Our Father has brought us home.

Notes

Preface

1. *Catechism of the Catholic Church*, 2nd ed. (United States Catholic Conference—Libreria Editrice Vaticana, 1997), 2777.

2. See John O'Donohue, *To Bless the Space Between Us: A Book of Blessings* (New York: Doubleday, 2008).

3. There are many issues and debates around different translations of the Lord's Prayer. We will use the translation of the *Catechism of the Catholic Church*, 2759.

4. John Shea, *The Spiritual Wisdom of the Gospels for Christian Preachers and Teachers* (Collegeville, MN: Liturgical Press, 2004, 2005, 2006, 2010).

Chapter One

1. *Jewish Folktales: Selected and Retold by Pinhas Sadeh* (New York: Doubleday, 1989), 396.

2. Christina Feldman and Jack Kornfield, eds., *Stories of the Spirit, Stories of the Heart: Parables of the Spiritual Path from Around the World* (San Francisco: HarperSanFrancisco, 1991), 25–26.

3. Frederick Denison Maurice, *The Lord's Prayer: Nine Sermons Preached in the Chapel of Lincoln's Inn* (Cambridge: Macmillan, 1861), Sermon 1.

Chapter Two

1. Rachel Naomi Remen, "Finding New Eyes," in *My Grandfather's Blessings: Stories of Strength, Refuge, and Belonging* (New York: Riverhead Books, 2000), 116–19.

2. Slightly modified from the version in Harry R. Moody and David Carroll, *The Five Stages of the Soul: Charting the Spiritual Passages That Shape Our Lives* (New York: Anchor Books, 1997), 197.

3. John Cobb, "Spiritual Discernment in a Whiteheadian Perspective," in *Religious Experience and Process Theology: The Pastoral Implications of a Major Modern Movement*, ed. Harry James Cargas and Bernard Lee (New York: Paulist Press, 1976).

4. T. S. Eliot, "East Coker," *Four Quartets* (New York: Harcourt, 1943), 28.

Chapter Three

1. Philip Novak, "The Dynamic of Attention in Discipline," in *Ultimate Reality and Spiritual Discipline*, ed. James Duerlinger (New York: Paragon House, 1984).

2. Susanna Hopton, quoted in Kenneth W. Stevenson, *The Lord's Prayer: A Text in Tradition* (Minneapolis: Fortress Press, 2004), 189.

3. Evelyn Underhill, *Abba: Meditations Based on the Lord's Prayer* (Essex, England: Longman Group, 1940).

4. Bede Griffiths, "Going Out of Oneself," *Parabola* 24, no. 2 (Summer 1999).

5. For example, see Ken Wilber, *Grace and Grit: Spirituality and Healing in the Life and Death of Treya Killam Wilber*, rev. ed. (Boston: Shambhala, 2000).

6. Robert Emmons, *The Psychology of Ultimate Concerns: Motivation and Spirituality in Personality* (New York: Guilford, 1999).

7. Ken Wilber, *Sex, Ecology, Spirituality: The Spirit of Evolution* (Boston: Shambhala, 1995), 414.

8. Kathleen Brehony, *After the Darkest Hour: How Suffering Begins the Journey to Wisdom* (New York: Henry Holt, 2000), 168–69.

9. Austin Farrer described the structure of the prayer as "three aspirations" and "three petitions." Consult Stevenson, *The Lord's Prayer*, 223.

10. See John Shea, *The Spiritual Wisdom of the Gospels for Christian Preachers and Teachers, Year C: The Relentless Widow* (Collegeville, MN: Liturgical Press, 2006), 207–14.

11. See John Dominic Crossan, *The Greatest Prayer: Rediscovering the Revolutionary Message of the Lord's Prayer* (New York: HarperOne, 2010).

12. For a profound meditation on the impact of ancestral faith, see Louis J. Cameli, *The Archaeology of Faith: A Personal Exploration of How We Come to Believe* (Notre Dame, IN: Ave Maria Press, 2015).

13. Charles Taylor, *A Secular Age* (Cambridge, MA: Belknap Press of Harvard University Press, 2007), 719.

14. Teresa of Ávila, *The Interior Castle*, quoted in Wilber, *Sex, Ecology, Spirituality*, 300.

15. Quoted in Robert K. C. Forman, *Meister Eckhart: Mystic as Theologian* (Germany: Element, 1991), 210.

16. Dietrich Bonhoeffer, *Life Together* (San Francisco: HarperSanFrancisco, 1993), 88.

17. Ken Wilber, *One Taste: Daily Reflections on Integral Spirituality* (Boston: Shambhala, 1999), 238–42.

18. Neil Douglas-Klotz, *Prayers of the Cosmos: Meditations on the Aramaic Words of Jesus* (San Francisco: HarperSanFrancisco, 1990).

Chapter Four

1. Jacob Needleman, *What Is God?* (New York: Jeremy P. Tarcher/ Penguin, 2009).

2. *World Spirituality: An Encyclopedic History of the Religious Quest* (The Crossroad Company, 1985), xiii.

3. Isaac the Syrian, quoted in Kallistos Ware, *The Orthodox Way*, rev. ed. (Crestwood, NY: St. Vladimir's Seminary Press, 1995), 55.

4. Walter Wink, *Naming the Powers: The Language of Power in the New Testament* (Minneapolis: Fortress Press, 1984), 119.

5. "Ah, not to be cut off," in *Ahead of All Parting: The Selected Poetry and Prose of Rainer Maria Rilke*, trans. Stephen Mitchell (New York: Modern Library, 1995), 191.

6. Kallistos Ware, "How do we enter the Heart?," in *Paths to the Heart: Sufism and the Christian East*, ed. James S. Cutsinger, 9 (Bloomington, IN: World Wisdom, 2002).

7. Ken Wilber, *Grace and Grit: Spirituality and Healing in the Life and Death of Treya Killam Wilber*, rev. ed. (Boston: Shambhala, 2000), 304.

8. Evelyn Underhill, "Our Two-Fold Relation to Reality," in *Evelyn Underhill: Modern Guide to the Ancient Quest for the Holy*, ed. Dana Greene (Albany, NY: State University of New York Press, 1988), 164–65.

9. Henry Suso, quoted in Kallistos Ware, *The Orthodox Way* (Crestwood, NY: St. Vladimir's Seminary Press, 1979), 119.

10. *The Theologia Germanica of Martin Luther*, trans. Bengt Hoffman (New York: Paulist Press, 1980), 64.

11. Remi Brague, "The Soul of Salvation," *Communio* 14 (Fall 1987): 226.

12. Quoted in Kenneth W. Stevenson, *The Lord's Prayer: A Text in Tradition* (Minneapolis: Fortress Press, 2004), 223.

13. Beatrice Bruteau, *The Holy Thursday Revolution* (Maryknoll, NY: Orbis Books, 2005), 54.

14. Cyprian Smith, *The Way of Paradox: Spiritual Life as Taught by Meister Eckhart* (London: Darton, Longman and Todd, 1987), 51.

15. Francis, *Laudato Si* (Vatican City: Libreria Editrice Vaticana, 2015) 89.

16. Thomas Merton, *Conjectures of a Guilty Bystander* (New York: Doubleday, 1966), 156–58.

17. *The Hidden Ground of Love: The Letters of Thomas Merton on Religious Experience and Social Concerns*, ed. William H. Shannon (New York: Farrar, Straus and Giroux, 1985).

18. *The Asian Journal of Thomas Merton* (New York: New Directions, 1973), 308.

19. Einstein, letter (1950), quoted in Silvan S. Schweber, *Einstein & Oppenheimer: The Meaning of Genius* (Cambridge, MA: Harvard University Press, 2008), 300.

20. Ken Wilber, *One Taste: Daily Reflections on Integral Spirituality* (Boston: Shambhala, 1999), 354–55.

21. *Thomas Merton: Essential Writings*, ed. Christine Bochen (Maryknoll, NY: Orbis Books, 2000), 38.

22. Ibid., 92, 40.

23. See, among others, "The Witness Exercise," in *The Essential Ken Wilber* (Boston: Shambhala, 1998); and *One Taste: The Journals of Ken Wilber* (Boston: Shambhala, 1999), 273–76; Cynthia Bourgeault, *Centering Prayer and Inner Awakening* (Cambridge, MA: Cowley, 2004); Grace Adolphsen Brame, *Receptive Prayer: A Christian Approach to Meditation* (St. Louis, MO: CBP Press, 1985); Eknath Easwaran, *Meditation: A Simple Eight-Point Program for Translating Spiritual Ideals into Daily Life* (Tomales, CA: Nilgiri Press, 1991); Dorothy Bass, ed., *Practicing Our Faith: A Guide for Conversation, Learning, and Growth* (San Francisco: Jossey-Bass, 1997); Yitzhak Buxbaum, *Jewish Spiritual Practices* (Northvale, NJ: J. Aronson, 1990); Anthony de Mello, *Sadhana, A Way to God: Christian Exercises in Eastern Form* (New York: Doubleday, 1984); Piero Ferrucci, *What We May Be: Techniques for Psychological and Spiritual Growth Through Psychosynthesis* (Los Angeles: J.P. Tarcher, 1982); Elizabeth Lesser, *The Seeker's Guide: Making Your Life a Spiritual Adventure* (New York: Random House, 2008); Roger Walsh, *Essential Spirituality: The 7 Central Practices to Awaken Heart and Mind* (New York: John Wiley, 1999); Philip Zaleski and Paul Kaufman, *Gifts of the Spirit: Living the Wisdom of the Great Religious Traditions* (San Francisco: HarperSanFrancisco, 1977).

24. Beatrice Bruteau, *The Holy Thursday Revolution* (Maryknoll, NY: Orbis Books, 2005), 71.

25. See Tim and Carol Flinders, *The Making of a Teacher: Conversations with Eknath Easwaran* (Petaluma, CA: Nilgiri Press, 1989).

26. Eknath Easwaran, *To Love Is to Know Me: The Bhagavad Gita for Daily Living*, vol. 3 (Petaluma, CA: Nilgiri Press, 1988), 9.

27. Rachel Naomi Remen, *My Grandfather's Blessings: Stories of Strength, Refuge, and Belonging* (New York: Riverhead Books, 2000), 23.

28. Ibid., 363–64.

29. Piero Ferrucci, *What We May Be: Techniques for Psychological and Spiritual Growth Through Psychosynthesis* (Los Angeles: J.P. Tarcher, 1982), 95–96.

30. Langdon Gilkey, *Gilkey on Tillich* (New York: Crossroad, 1990), 97.

31. W. H. Auden, *For the Time Being* (Princeton, NJ: Princeton University Press, 2013), 65.

Chapter Five

1. "As kingfishers catch fire," in *Gerard Manley Hopkins*, ed. Catherine Phillips (Oxford: Oxford University Press, 1986), 129.

2. Stephen H. Ruppenthal, trans., "Discourse on Good Will," in *The Path of Direct Awakening: Passages for Meditation* (Berkeley, CA: Berkeley Hills, 2004), as quoted in Eknath Easwaran, *God Makes the Rivers to Flow: An Anthology of the World's Sacred Poetry & Prose* (Tomales, CA: Nilgiri Press, 1991), 104–5.

3. Rachel Naomi Remen, *Kitchen Table Wisdom: Stories That Heal* (New York: Riverhead Books, 1996), 78–80.

4. See Robert Barron, *The Priority of Christ: Toward a Postliberal Catholicism* (Grand Rapids, MI: Brazos Press, 2007), 192.

5. Quoted in Beatrice Bruteau, *The Holy Thursday Revolution* (Maryknoll, NY: Orbis Books, 2005), 54.

6. See Bernard McGinn, *The Mystical Thought of Meister Eckhart: The Man from Whom God Hid Nothing* (New York: Crossroad, 2001), 48.

7. Abraham Joshua Heschel, *Man Is Not Alone: A Philosophy of Religion* (New York: Farrar, Straus and Giroux, 1951), 20.

8. Christian Wiman, *My Bright Abyss: Meditation of a Modern Believer* (New York: Farrar, Straus and Giroux, 2013), 116.

9. R. S. Thomas, "The Coming," in *R. S. Thomas*, ed. Anthony Thwaite, Everyman's Poetry (London: J.M. Dent, 1996), 72.

10. John Dominic Crossan and Marcus Borg, *The Last Week* (New York: HarperCollins, 2006), 3.

11. See John Shea, *The Spiritual Wisdom of the Gospels for Christian Preachers and Teachers: On Earth as It Is in Heaven, Year A* (Collegeville, MN: Liturgical Press, 2004), 103–7; *The Spiritual Wisdom of the Gospels for Christian Preachers and Teachers: The Relentless Widow, Year C* (2006), 63–69.

12. See Shea, "Wearing Down Injustice," in *Spiritual Wisdom of the Gospels, Year C*, 289–93.

13. Alfred North Whitehead, *Religion in the Making* (New York: Cambridge University Press, 1926), 60–61.

14. Elizabeth Barrett Browning, *Aurora Leigh and Other Poems* (New York: Penguin Books, 1995), 467.

15. Nikos Kazantzakis, *Report to Greco*, trans. P. A. Bien (New York: Simon and Schuster, 1965), 50.

16. Rachel Naomi Remen, *My Grandfather's Blessings: Stories of Strength, Refuge, and Belonging* (New York: Riverhead Books, 2000), 247.

17. Alan Ecclestone, *Yes to God* (St. Meinrad, IN: Abbey Press, 1975).

Chapter Six

1. For a detailed reading of these texts see John Dominic Crossan, *The Greatest Prayer: Rediscovering the Revolutionary Message of the Lord's Prayer* (New York: HarperCollins, 2010).

2. See the spiritual teaching story "Turning the Wheel" in chapter 2.

3. For a longer and more detailed exposition of this story, see John Shea, *The Spiritual Wisdom of the Gospels for Christian Preachers and Teachers: On Earth as It Is in Heaven, Year A* (Collegeville, MN: Liturgical Press, 2004), 272–78.

4. Joy Williams, *Ninety-Nine Stories of God* (Portland, OR: Tin House Books, 2016), 100.

5. Beatrice Bruteau, *The Grand Option: Personal Transformation and a New Creation* (Notre Dame: University of Notre Dame Press, 2001), 134.

6. For a longer and more detailed exposition of these temptation narratives, see Shea, *Spiritual Wisdom of the Gospels, Year A*, 103–7; *Year B*, 79–80; *Year C*, 63–69.

7. For a detailed interpretation of this story, see Shea, *Spiritual Wisdom of the Gospels for Christian Preachers and Teachers: Following Love into Mystery; Feasts, Funerals, and Weddings* (Collegeville, MN: Liturgical Press, 2010), 104–10.

Chapter Seven

1. Isa 11:2-3 (wisdom, understanding, counsel, fortitude, knowledge, piety, fear of the Lord); 1 Cor 12:8-10 (expression of wisdom, expression of knowledge, faith, healing, miracles, prophecy, discerning spirits, speaking in tongues, interpretation of tongues); Gal 5:22-23 (charity, joy, peace, patience, kindness, goodness, long-suffering, humility, fidelity, modesty, continence, chastity).

2. See Robert Barron, *The Priority of Christ: Toward a Postliberal Catholicism* (Grand Rapids, MI: Brazos Press, 2007), part V: The Display of Christian Form.

3. T. S. Eliot, *Murder in the Cathedral* (Orlando, FL: Harcourt, 1935), 19.